# Names

## for Your

# Baby

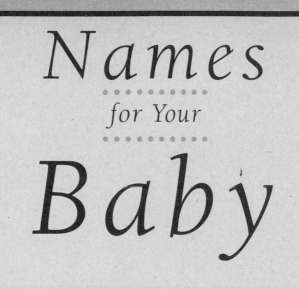

# Names
### for Your
# Baby

Compiled by the editors of
*American Baby Names*

*Wings Books*
*New York • Avenel, New Jersey*

This 1995 edition is published by Wings Books, distributed by Random House Value Publishing, Inc., 40 Engelhard Avenue, Avenel, New Jersey 07001, by arrangement with American Baby Books, Inc.

Random House
New York • Toronto • London • Sydney • Auckland

Printed and bound in the United States of America

Library of Congress Cataloging–in–Publication Data

Names for your baby / compiled by the editors of American Baby Books.
     p.  cm.
    First published: Wauwatosa, WI : American Baby Books, c1981.
    ISBN 0–517–35622–8
    1. Names, Personal—Dictionaries. I. American Baby Books (Firm) II. Title.
CS2377.W53 1995                  95–14840
929.4'4'0973—dc20             CIP

# Contents

# *Introduction*

● ● ● ● ● ● ● ● ● ● ●

As Shakespeare said so memorably, "A rose by any other name would smell as sweet." But twentieth century psychologists and sociologists present a different view, perhaps best summarized as: "A rose by any other name would *sound less sweet.*"

There is *magic* in a name.

What parents have long suspected has been proven true in formal studies: Children with names like Claude and Gladys are perceived less favorably than youngsters with identities more melodically labeled, for example, Melanie or Michael. And in turn, these unfortunately designated children tend to have poorer self-images than their more popularly named counterparts.

*Names do count*...throughout their bearers' lives and often beyond. Philosophers have said the nature and character of things are condensed and represented in their names. And the act of "naming" is believed to be the earliest of all intellectual accomplishments.

The primary purpose of this book is to provide parents-to-be with *inspiration* throughout the process of naming their babies. The names you give your children will be the first gifts you present them...and the most lasting. So the tradition of naming certainly deserves the time and attention you are now granting it.

We'll do our part by offering in these pages all we know about the history of the name game.

The most important information provided within *Names For Your Baby* is, of course, the "dictionary" of girls' and boys' names, their origins and meanings. This is where your creativity is put to the test. Try out your favorites with your surname. Write them down, then speak them aloud. How do they sound together? You—and only you—will know which name is right for the beloved new member of your family.

Use of the dictionary is easy to master. Following each name is its origin and translation as it was literally understood by natives of the originating country. Almost all common Christian names are derived from one of five language families: Hebrew, Greek, Latin, Celtic, and Teutonic. Generally, Hebrew names generally relate to deity; Teutonic names emphasize warlike terms and qualities; Greek, Latin, and Celtic names usually refer to abstract qualities and personal characteristics.

Following each name is a number of its "derivatives": in some cases, they're quite different in sound and spelling. (Ex.: Adelaide—Heidi.) "Curiosities" have been culled and purposefully omitted, for we believe that few parents would consider them—and fewer children would enjoy "owning" them.

Choosing a name for a child is one of the most enjoyable decisions a parent will make. So savor these precious moments...and proceed with pleasure.

Congratulations & best wishes,
The Editors

# Chapter 1

# What's Behind A Name:

## The History

First or "given," names were used to identify a person long before individuals had both first and last names. They were bestowed upon converts to Christianity at their baptismal ceremonies, so were also designated "christened" names. (The term "Christian" name is a deviation from the correct description, "christened" name.)

Surnames (last names) were regarded as "family names" and came into general use about 1100 A.D. in England, then throughout Europe.

From the first, the church assumed a key role in naming babies, decreeing that only the names of saints and martyrs could be given at baptism. Families derived some comfort from this custom, since they believed their children's hallowed namesakes would protect and support them—a welcome thought as most were struggling to wrest a meager living from the soil.

Even as late as the sixteenth century, the Church of England continued to prohibit the naming of children after "heathen gods." Nothing less than a saint or martyr would do. And since a priest's presence was required at the rights of baptism and confirmation, the Church would ensure that its rules were obeyed. Even now, at baptism and in marriage ceremonies, only one name—the christened one—is used.

Original English names were drawn chiefly from the Anglo-Saxon language. Norman names, mostly of Teutonic origin, were bequeathed to us as a direct result of the Norman Conquest of England in 1066.

Twenty years later, William the Conqueror launched a primitive but serious attempt to document "Who's Who" and Who's Where" in England. His challenging undertaking, referred to as the *Domesday Book* and encompassing all of that country's population, was a pet project because it ascertained his fiscal rights as a king. (Owners of vast estates were taxed for their workers as well as their land.) The names recorded showed that society then relied almost entirely on a repertoire of 20 names for each sex. About four-fifths of the men were called John, William, Thomas, Richard, Robert, or Henry. The rest were named Roger, Walter, Hugh, Rolf, Edmund, Nicholas, or Philip.

Women were named Agnes, Alice, Cicely, Joan, Matilda, Margaret, Elizabeth, Isabel, Helen, Elaine, Emme, Katherine, Mabel, Sibyl, or Beatrice.

The perennial popularity of these names is obvious from just a brief review of surnames derived from them: John is represented by Jones, Johnson (derived from "son of John"), Johnston, Jenkins, and Jackson. William produced Williams, Williamson, Wilson, Wills, Gill, and

Wilkens. Thomas has presented us Thompson, Thomson, Tomkins; and from Richard, we have Richardson, Rickert, and Dickson.

Naturally, the meager supply of first names was reflected in an equally limited choice of surnames. When offspring did not elect to use the customary "son of" or "daughter of" John or William or Thomas, last names were often chosen to reflect the work of the people who lived in the medieval manors and towns, bringing us such common names as Smith, Miller, and Cook. Others took their last names from their home-places, a custom that afforded us those like Britton (from Britain), Flanders, and Cornwall—plus a multitude of their derivatives.

In the names of men and women today are mirrored the struggles, ambitions, and aspirations of ancient villagers, the habits and work of townspeople, and the daily life of both noble and ignoble.

What's in a name?

*Humanity*...and nothing less.

# Chapter 2

# What's In A Name:
## The Psychology

People generally like—or dislike—certain names as a result of their experiences with persons "labeled" as such. If a fondly remembered childhood pal was known as Sigismunda, it will always seem a melodious title to us. Likewise, if the street corner bully was called Raoul, the name will forever bear negative connotations.

It is also common knowledge that familiar names are more likely to be preferred to those that sound foreign to the ear. This inequitable but understandable phenomenon makes it difficult for strangers with unusual names to be taken at face value. Immigrants to this country quickly learned this sad fact. While they could do little about their own names, they "Americanized" the designations of their offspring, often even changing and abridging their surnames. (Fortunately, this custom is steadily changing, now that many people are taking new pride in their ethnic background and naming their children accordingly.)

Research discloses, too, that people generally prefer names that are most popular at the moment. It is not surprising, then, to find statistics show that the majority of people who express dissatisfaction with their names possess those considered "uncommon."

After all, the mere "sound" of a name can have great impact on its owner's life. Ever hear of William Dawes? It's unlikely that you have, yet he rode with Paul Revere to Lexington "that Eighteenth of April, in Seventy-Five," to warn fellow citizens the British were coming. It was Dawes in fact who actually made it through enemy lines to accomplish the task of alerting his countrymen; Revere was captured by British soldiers and never reached Lexington.

So why did Longfellow immortalize Revere and ignore Dawes in his celebrated poem, "The Midnight Ride of Paul Revere"? The name Paul Revere offered more of a "musical lilt" than William Dawes, lending itself better to rhyme!

Even before that, the New World had been named after explorer Amerigo Vespucci, although historians contend that he never saw the American continent. An unheralded, obscure mapmaker named Martin Waldseemuller suggested the name America, and so labeled that part of the Western Hemisphere. But for a quirk of fate, patriotic citizens might now be concluding their gatherings with a round of a stirring melody entitled "Waldseemullerland, the Beautiful."

And when Carry Amelia Moore married Mr. Nation and adopted his surname, her new name—Carry A. Nation—prompted her to act on her convictions concerning alcohol, for she believed she had been fated to "Carry A Nation" to prohibition. (Aided by the incongruous combination of psalms and hatchets—and like-minded ladies—she did!)

It was no accident, either, that the author Charles Dickens so aptly named the notorious characters from his most beloved books. Scrooge, Blathers, and Bumble were indeed descriptive titles. And wasn't Mr. Micawber every bit as unpleasant as his name suggested?

A name calls forth, in imagery, a portrait of a person. Though it may be implausible, many of us form mental images of people who answer to certain names before we have even met them.

Take Betty, for instance. Upon hearing the name, do you envision Betty Ford, Betty Grable, or Betty Furness? What about the popular name John? Perhaps you immediately entertain a mental picture of that charismatic president John Kennedy...of former Beatle John Lennon, who met the same tragic fate...or even John Wayne, if you're a "wild western" buff.

There are thousands of Jims, Bobs, Joans, and Janes. And those you have known become part of the mental "association" created each time you hear the name.

"Unreasonable and irrational," you may say. Unquestionably! But true, nonetheless.

This phenomenon has even been noted half a world away. Some African tribes habitually name their children after the day of the week upon which they are born, believing the youngsters' personalities can be categorized accordingly. "Wednesday's child," they say, is aggressive and quarrelsome; "Monday's" is quiet and peace loving. Is it any wonder, then, that court records from these tribal communities show twice as many "Wednesday children" arrested as those born on Monday? These babies' destinies may very well be predetermined—but by peoples' preconceived notions about them, not by their day of birth!

In the nebulous area of names, there are exceptions to every "rule." So if you've already fallen in love with a name and you sincerely believe it will be right for your child, you're well-advised to *follow your heart.*

# Chapter 3

# Names:
# The
# Determining
# Factors

Now it is down to *business*—The business of naming your child, that is. And inspiration is forthcoming in these popular methods of decision making:

*Honoring a relative.* If you choose to make your child the "namesake" of a favorite grandparent, aunt, uncle, or any other ancestor, you are in good company. About 60 percent of all American babies are named after close relatives. If you are a woman who has adopted her husband's surname, you may want to consider, too, calling your child by your maiden name.

Of course, your fondest desire may be to bequeath your child your name—or that of your spouse. A time-honored tradition it is...and one that may mean much to both of you through the years. But give some thought to what you'll actually call the child to eliminate confusion in your household. A boy named after his father, John, might be dubbed Jack, for instance; a girl named after her mother, Margaret, could be called by the nickname Meg.

If you have titles of two people you wish to honor with your baby's name, why not combine syllables from each and create a name? James and John meld beautifully into Jason; even George and Jean are lovely together as Gena.

*Honoring a celebrated person.* Many a John Fitzgerald was christened in the 1960s. And Elizabeth is, understandably, a popular name among English children. If you have a hero or heroine whom you admire and his/her name is pleasing when pronounced alongside your surname, you are a step ahead in the naming game. Just be certain the personality you are honoring won't become embarrassingly controversial in the years ahead. (One hopes there weren't too many Benedict Arnolds around in the late 1800s.)

*Honoring ethnic heritage.* As mentioned in Chapter Two, Americans previously sought to change names obviously of ethnic origin. Fortunately, this custom is changing now that more and more people are expressing interest and pride in their "roots." The results are some utterly lyrical names for children, as exemplified here:

*Greek*: Talia, Delia, Dorian.

*Hebrew*: Leah, Noah, Reuben.

*Irish*: Kelly, Moira, Sean.

*Spanish*: Maria, Delores, Miguel.

*Scandinavian*: Dagmar, Arla, Bjorn.

*Turkish*: Ali, Halim, Halil.

*Honoring an aspiration or ideal.* Names such as Faith, Grace, Hope, and Bliss significantly express parents' love for and belief in their children.

*Signifying a circumstance of birth.* April, May, Tuesday, Noel, Christmas, and Summer are pretty—and self-explanatory—names. Even the child's birthplace can be a source of a distinctive name, as in Madison, Ames, and Dover.

*Choosing a "unisex" name.* Many parents prefer "unisex" names like Robin, Lynn, Lindsey, Drew, Leslie, Tony, or Sydney. Each of these titles is distinctive and may, indeed, eliminate the risk of sex bias in some situations. But if this is the course you choose, be aware that your child is likely to receive mail and official documents addressing him/her in the wrong gender and that other such confusion is likely to prevail.

*Creating an "anagram."* If you have a knack for concocting anagrams—transpositions of the letters to make new words—you may want to fashion your child's names from a word that has special significance for you: Caepe from "peace," for example.

Now is the time to allow your full creativity rein. In fact, you may feel ready to turn to the dictionary of girls' and boys' names and add to your list of favorites. Once you've collected a few titles that particularly appeal to you, see if they stand up to these "tests":

*Will this name be appropriate when my child is middle-aged?* Cissy or Dickie are cute names for babies and young children, but they will not wear well with age. (Some members of African tribes present their babies with names at birth, then replace them with new ones when the children reach maturity.)

*Is this name difficult to spell or pronounce?* One of the principle reasons some Americans legally change their names is to put an end to lengthy explanations regarding the pronunciation and spelling of particularly uncommon ones. Have a heart when it comes to this aspect of the title your child will live with. Hephzibah may appeal to you, but who can spell it...much less pronounce it?

*Have you inadvertently created a rhyme or "elision" (name that forms a phrase when spoken along with the surname)?* No matter how you look at it, it is not fun to go through life with a name like Norman Gorman or Imin Pain. Take every precaution to avoid these pitfalls.

*Will you like nicknames derived from this name?* Kids love to call each other by pet names, so forego the title of Henry if its common "diminuitive," Hank, is anathema to you. If, on the other hand, you are choosing a name because you love its common nickname, why not skip the formalities and have the diminuitive officially entered on the child's birth certificate? Consider, too, using a contemporary spelling of a nickname. In most cases, that involves ending the name with an "i" in lieu of "y" or "ie"—as in Mari, Toni, and Joni.

*Does the name blend euphoniously and rhythmically with your surname?* Generally, a hyphenated surname or one with two or more syllables sounds best with a short given name, while a single-syllable last name requires a longer accompaniment. Examples are Drew Masterson; Christopher Jones. And try not to chose a first name that ends with a vowel if your surname begins with one—Nora Oren is just not melodic.

## And A Few
## Words About Middle Names

Only three of the first presidents of the United States had middle names. It was rare, in fact, for anyone to be graced with more than one given name until about 1750. But now that our population has multiplied many times over and computer technology requires specific identification per individual, it is a rarity for a baby not to be given a middle name at birth. (The army and navy generally proffer the undignified abbreviation "NMI"—no middle initial—when a recruit's parents have not presented this third title to him/her.)

When selecting a middle name, two simple guidelines can help. First, keep it euphoniously and rhythmically "in tune" with the given and surnames—brief if they are long and vice-versa. Examples are Katherine Ann Collingwood; Mark Huntington Smith. Then, take care that the three initials do not form an embarrassing word, such as "HAG" or "SAD." While this may seem a minor point, it can cause such a person to shy away from monograms the rest of his/her life.

Finally, a woman who uses her husband's surname as her own may wish to give their child her maiden name as a middle title. These are often beautiful and distinctive complements to a given name as well as thoughtful remembrances of the baby's maternal grandparents.

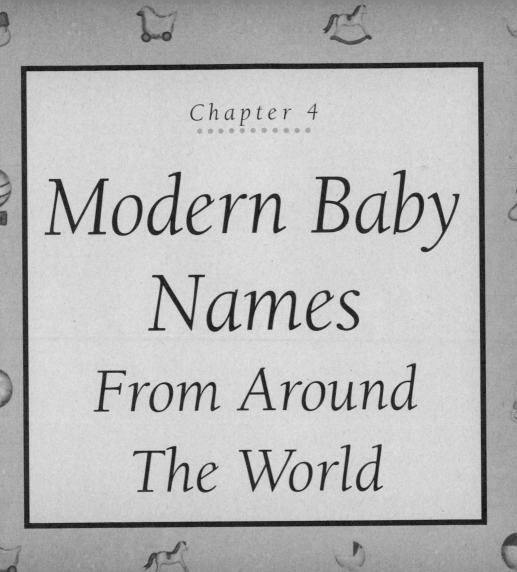

Chapter 4

# Modern Baby Names
## From Around The World

Like last year's swimsuit, the world seems somehow to have "shrunk."

This age of electronic communication—and our "takeover" by TV, in particular—have thrust previously remote areas of the earth right into our living rooms. Simultaneously, supersonic transport quickly deposits American travelers anywhere in the world within hours.

So from either television or personal observation, people today know about other people. They know what they do...how they live...and what their names are. Consequently, titles that might once have sounded curious or exotic have melded into the American cultural milieu.

It is fortunate, then, that so many of these ethnic names are significant and lyrically lovely. They also embody centuries of history and tradition and can, therefore, be a source of pride for a child.

A collection of beautiful names from other lands follows—one specifically for girls, another for boys. Choose carefully if this idea appeals to you.

All titles are considered traditional in their originating countries; most are now gaining popularity in the United States. Many of the names will "fit" perfectly with your surname, while others might need some slight revision to achieve a euphonious blend.

It's appropriate that American children bear names from all nations. After all, excluding the American Indians, every citizen of this country is closely descended from another country.

# Girls

| | | | |
|---|---|---|---|
| Aimee | Danett | Hillary | Kasi |
| Alana | Dede | Holly | Kelsy (i) |
| Ali | Dina | Ilana | Kisa |
| Ami | Dodie | Ivy | Kori |
| Bel | Doni | Jahaira | Kristin |
| Bina | Edi | Jani | Lani |
| Birgit | Elli | Jenna | Lara |
| Bo | Franci | Jerika | Laure |
| Brooke | Gari | Joana | Lea |
| Byleshia | Germaine | Joby (i) | Lenni |
| Cam | Gina | Kala (i) | Lian (Lianna) |
| Cara | Ginger | Kalle (ie) | Lexie |
| Carly | Greer | Kane | Lotti |
| Cesta | Halli | Kari | Mara (i) |
| Cher | Harper | Karli | Marni |
| Dacy | Heather | Karma | Marva |

| | | | |
|---|---|---|---|
| Mega | Pilar | Suki | Veda |
| Michi | Poni | Suzu | Viki |
| Miki | Priya | Tala | Willow |
| Miryan | Randi | Tami (my) | Windi (a) |
| Missie | Rea | Tara | Yoki |
| Mona | Ren | Tawnie | Yori |
| Mylyn | Reva | Teri | Yvette |
| Nani | Rin | Timmi | Zanette |
| Neely | Ruana | Tori | Zita |
| Neva | Ruri | Towhee | Zuri |
| Niki | Sabra | Trella | |
| Nita | Sacha (i) | Trini (a) | |
| Nori | Sen | Tristin | |
| Ona (i) | Shalamar | Tyreshida | |
| Patti | Shani | Tyshawana | |
| Penni | Shira | Valli | |

## *Boys*

| | | | |
|---|---|---|---|
| Adar | Bane | Caton | Davin |
| Adel | Beck | Chad | Deke |
| Adri | Bem | Chaim | Dion |
| Alain | Berdy | Chase | Dore (i) |
| Alek | Berk | Cham | Doyle |
| Ali | Birk | Chi | Duff |
| Alrik | Blaze | Chik | Dade |
| Angel (o) | Bond (on) | Clay | Dustin |
| Archer | Bram | Colman | Dylan |
| Arel | Brandeis | Cowan | Dyshaun |
| Ari | Brody | Cris | Edan |
| Arley (i) | Burr | Dagan | Erin |
| Ash | Cam | Degan | Faber |
| Avi | Carlos | Dane | Fin (n) |
| Balin | Catalin | Dar | Flint |

| | | | |
|---|---|---|---|
| Franco | Kane | Nari | Slade |
| Garth | Kass (Cass) | Odin (on) | Tad |
| Hale | Keddy | Pal | Tait |
| Hanan | Keegan | Pattin | Tano |
| Hari | Keir | Purdy | Tate |
| Hod (d) | Kell (y) | Ranon | Tem |
| Hollis | Keri | Rene | Timur |
| Holt | Kim | Robi | Tomi |
| Hurley | Kriss | Roth | Tymon |
| Jacy | Kyle | Rud | Van |
| Javier | Lenn | Sani | Wen |
| Jay | Mato | Sef | Yancy |
| Jed | Mikkel | Shanon | Yary (i) |
| Jin | Morgan | Shem | Yves |
| Jari | Nigan | Shen | Zeki |

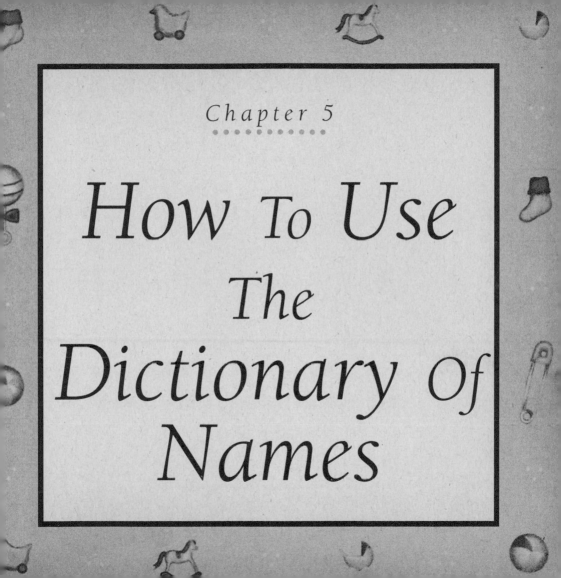

Chapter 5

# How To Use The Dictionary Of Names

You will find the following two dictionaries easy to use. The first includes titles traditionally deemed girls'; the second is chock-full of boys' names. Note, too, the many entries in each with both masculine and feminine forms. Now it is simple to name a boy after his mother or a girl after her father—choose a variation of the title that reflects the gender of the child.

For "memory insurance," mark or make a list of the names that seem...somehow...magically right. They are listed alphabetically on the left sides of the pages. Beside each is its origin (in parentheses), then its literal meaning in the native language. (Remember: these are definitions of the name—not a child!)

Finally, each name is followed by those derived from it. If you can't immediately find a particular name, look for one that is similar to it and read through its derivatives. The name you seek may be a variation of another.

"Listen" to your imagination as you read and consider each name as it might apply to your little one. Will she be alert...a "seeker" from the moment she is born? Will his smile be "as the sun"?

Happy reading—and good luck.

# Chapter 6

## *Girl's Names*

*Abigail* (Hebrew) "a source of great joy"; wife of King David. Abbe, Abbey, Abbi, Abbie, Abby, Abigael, Gael, Gale, Gayle, Gail.

*Abra* (Hebrew) "mother of many notions." Abira, Avra.

*Acacia* (Greek) "thorny." Cacia, Casey, Casia.

*Ada* (Teutonic) "prosperous; happy." Short form of Adelaide, Adda, Addie, Adi, Aida.

*Adelaide* (Teutonic) "noble and of good cheer." Addie, Addy, Adel, Adela, Adele, Adeline, Adelle, Aline, Del, Della, Ellie, Elsie, Elsa, Heidi.

*Adeline* English form of Adelaide.

*Adele* French form of Adelaide.

*Adina* (Hebrew) "delicate." Adena, Dena, Dina.

*Adora* (Latin) "beloved." Dora, Dori, Dorie.

*Adrienne* (Latin) "dark; rich." Adrea, Adira, Adrianna, Adriane, Hadra.

*Agatha* (Greek) "the good." Agace, Agathe, Aggie, Aggy.

*Agnes* (Greek) "pure; gentle; meek." Ag, Aggie, Agna, Agnella, Annis, Ina, Innes, Inez, Nessa, Nessie, Nessy, Una, Ynez.

*Aidan* (Irish Gaelic) "little fiery one." Aidan, Edan.

*Aileen* (Irish Gaelic) "light." Irish form of Helen. Aila, Ailene, Aleen, Eileen, Eleen, Llene, Lena, Lina.

*Aimee* French form of Amy.

*Alanna* (Irish Gaelic) "fair; comely." A feminine form of Alan. Alana, Alaine, Alleen, Allina, Allyn, Lana.

*Alberta* (Teutonic) "noble and brilliant." A feminine form of Albert, Albertina, Albertine, Ali, Allie, Alverta, Bert, Berta, Bertie, Elberta, Elbertina, Elbertine.

*Alcina* (Greek) "strong-minded."

*Alda* (Teutonic) "rich."

*Aldora* (Greek) "winged gift."

*Alexandra* (Greek) "helper of mankind." Feminine form of Alexander. Alessandra, Alexa, Alexandrina, Alexina, Alexine, Alexis, Ali, Alix, Allie, Allix, Elana, Lesya, Lexi, Sandra, Sandy, Sondra, Zandra.

*Alfreda* (Teutonic) "supernaturally wise." Feminine form of Alfred. Alfie, Alfy, Elfreda, Elfrida, Elva, Freda, Freddie, Freida.

*Ali* Short form of Alexandra or Alice.

*Alice* (Greek) "truth"; (Teutonic) "noble." Adelice, Aleece, Alicia, Alisa, Alison, Alissa, Allie, Allison, Allyce, Alysia, Alyssa, Elissa, Llysa, Lissa.

*Alicia* English form of Alice.

*Allegra* (Latin) "sprightly; cheerful."

*Allison* (Greek) "little; truthful"; (Teutonic) "famous among the gods."

Irish form of Alice.  Ali, Alisha, Alison, Alyson, Allie, Alyssia, Lissy.

*Alma* (Arabic) "learned."

*Althea* (Greek) "wholesome; healing."  Elthea, Thea.

*Alvina* (Teutonic) "beloved by all."  Feminine form of Alvin.  Vina,
Vinnie, Vinny.

*Alvita* (Latin) "vivacious, animated."

*Alyssa* (Greek) "sane, logical."

*Amabel* (Latin) "lovable."  Amabelle, Bel

*Amanda* (Latin) "lovable."  Manda, Mandy.

*Amara* (Greek) "of eternal beauty; unfading."  Mara.

*Amber* (Arabic) "amber."  As in the semi-precious jewel purported  to
have curative properties.

*Amelia* (Latin) "industrious."  Amalia, Amelie, Amelina, Ameline, Amy.

*Amelinda* (Latin) "beloved; pretty."  Linda, Melina.

*Amity* (Latin) "friendship."

*Amy* (Latin) "beloved."  Aimee, Ame, Ami, Esma, Esme.

*Anastasia* (Greek) "of the Resurretion; of springtime."  Ana, Ann,
Anna, Anastassia, Stacey, Stacie, Stacy, Tasia.

*Andrea* (Latin) "womanly."  Feminine form of Andrew.  Andi,
Andreanna, Andree, Andria, Andrianna, Andy.

*Angela* (Greek) "the heavenly messenger."  Angel, Angelica, Angelina,
Angeline, Angelique, Angelita, Angie.

*Anita* Spanish familiar form of Ann.

*Ann, Anne* (Hebrew) "graceful; mercy or prayer."  An English form of

Hannah.  Ana, Anette, Anica, Anita, Anna, Annabella, Anabelle, Annetta, Annie, Annis, Anushka, Anya, Hannah, Hanni, Nan, Nana, Nance, Nancy, Nanette, Nanine, Nanni, Nanon, Nettie, Nina,  Nita.

*Annabel* (Latin) "lovable one."  Annabella, Annabella.

*Annette* Familiar form of Ann.

*Antoinette* (Latin) "priceless."  A feminine form of Anthony.  Antonetta, Antonia, Antonie, Antonietta, Netta, Netti, Nettie, Toni, Tonia, Tonie.

*April* (Latin) "opening."  Apriltte, Avril.

*Arabella* (Latin) "beautiful altar."  Arabelle, Bella, Belle.

*Ardelle* (Latin) "ardent; zealous."  Ardeen, Addelia, Ardelis, Ardella, Ardene, Ardine.

*Ardis* (Latin) "fervent or eager"; (Teutonic) "rich gift."

*Aretha* (Greek) "best."  Aretta, Oretha, Retha.

*Aretina* (Greek) "virtuous."

*Ariel* (Hebrew) "lion of God."  Ariella, Arielle.

*Arlene* (Celtic) "pledge."  Feminine form of Arlen.  Arlana, Arleen, Ariena, Arieta, Arlette.

*Arva* (Latin) "fertile."

*Ashley* (Old Englsih) "of the ash-tree."  Ash, Ashely.

*Astra* (Greek) "starlike."

*Astrid* (Teutonic) "impulsive in love."

*Atalanta* (Greek) "swift huntress."  Atlanta.

*Atalaya* (Spanish-Arabic) "a watch tower."

*Athena* (Greek) "wisdom.

*Auberta* (Teutonic) "noble; brilliant."

*Audrey* ( Teutonic) "noble; strong."  Audi, Audie, Audra, Audrie, Audry.

*Augusta* (Latin) "exhalted, sublime."  Feminine form of Augustus, Augustina, Augustine, Austine, Gussie, Gussy, Tina.

*Aurelia* (Latin) "golden."  Aurelea, Aurora, Ora, Oralee, Orel, Orelee, Orelia.

*Aurora* (Latin) "dawn."  Ora, Rori, Rory.

*Ava* (Latin) "birdlike."

*Avery* (Old English) "small, wise counselor."

*Avis* (Teutonic) "refuge in battle."

*Avita* (Latin) "birdlike."

*Aviva* (Hebrew) "springtime."  Viva.

*Azelin* (Hebrew) "spared by Jehovah."

*Bambi* (Italian) "baby; child." Short for Bambino.

*Barbara* (Latin) "the stranger." Babette, Babs, Barb, Barbe, Barbee, Barbi, Barbie, Barbra, Barby, Bobbee, Bobbi, Bobby, Bonni, Bonnie, Bonny, Varina.

*Basilia* (Greek) "regal one." Basile.

*Bathsheba* (Hebrew) "daughter of the oath."

*Beatrice* (Latin) "she who makes happy." Bea, Beatrix, Bebe, Bee, Trix, Trixie.

*Becky* (Hebrew) "the ensnarer." Familiar form of Rebecca.

*Belinda* (Spanish) "beautiful." Name popularized by Alexander Pope (*The Rape of the Lock*). Linda, Lyn, Lynn.

*Bella* (Latin) "beautiful."

*Belle* (French) "beautiful." Bell, Bella, Billie, Billy.

*Benita* (Latin) "blessed." Benedetta, Benedicta, Benni, Binnie.

*Bernadine* (French) "brave warrior." Bernadene, Bernadette, Bernadina, Bernadine, Bernetta, Bernette, Bernie.

*Bernice* (Greek) "bringer of victory." Berni, Bunni, Bunnie, Bunny, Veronica.

*Bertha* (Teutonic) "bright or glorious." Berta, Bertie, Bertina.

*Bertina* (Teutonic) "shining."

*Beryl* (Greek) "a jewel."

*Beth* (Hebrew) "house of God." Short form of Elizabeth. Bethany, Bethena, Bethia.

*Betsy, Bette, Betty, Bessie* Familiar forms of Elizabeth.

*Bettina* (Hewbrew) "consecrated to God."

*Beulah* (Hebrew) "married."

*Beverly* (Teutonic) "from the beaver-meadow." Bev, Buffy, Verlie.

*Bionca* (Italian) Form of Blanche, Blonca.

*Billie* (Teutonic) "strong-willed." Billy.

*Blaine* (Irish Gaelic) "slender one."

*Blair* (Scottish Gaelic) "from the fields."

*Blanche* (Teutonic-Latin) "white; fair." Bellanca, Bianca, Blanch, Blinni.

*Blanda* (Latin) "affable; flattering."

*Blossom* (Modern) "flower-like."

*Blythe* (Anglo-Saxon) "joyous." Blithe.

*Bonita* (Spanish) "pretty."

*Bonnie, Bonny* (French-Latin) "sweet; fair."

*Brenda* (Teutonic) "fire-brand."

*Brenna* (Celtic) "raven; maid."

*Brett* (Celtic) "from Britain."

*Briana* (Irish Gaelic) "strong."  Feminine form of Brian.  Brina, Briney.

*Bridget* (Celtic) "resolute strength."  Biddy, Birgit, Birgitta, Brigid, Brigida, Brigitta, Brigitte, Brita.

*Brittany* (Latin) "from England."  Britt, Britta.

*Brooke* (Teutonic) "from the brook."

*Brumhilda* (Teutonic) "armored battle-maid."  Brunhilde, Hilda, Hilde.

*Caitlin* (Irish Gaelic) Form of Catherine.

*Calandra* (Greek) "lark." Cal, Calandria, Calli, Callie.

*Calida* (Spanish) "ardent."

*Calla* (Greek) "beautiful." Call, Callie.

*Callista* (Greek) "most beautiful." Calesta, Calista, Calli, Cally.

*Calvina* Latin feminine form of Calvin.

*Camille* (Latin) "young ceremonial attendant." Cam, Camila, Camilla, Cammie, Millie, Milly.

*Candace* (Greek) "glittering; flowing white." Candi, Candice, Candie, Candis, Candy, Kandy.

*Candida* (Latin) "pure white." Candi, Candide, Candy.

*Cara* (Celtic) "friend"; (Latin) "dear." Carina, Carine, Carrie.

*Cari* (Turkish) "flows like water."

*Carina* (Latin) "keel." Carin, Carine.

*Carisa* (Latin) "artful."

*Carita* (Latin) "charitable."

*Carla* Teutonic feminine form of Charles. "a strong country woman."

*Carlie* Familiar form of Caroline, Charlotte.

*Carlotta* Italian form of Charlotte.

*Camel* (Hebrew) "woodland; park." Carmela, Carmelita, Lita.

*Carmen* (Latin) "song"; (Spanish) "from Mount Carmel." Carma, Carmencita, Carmina, Carmine, Charmaine.

*Carol* (Latin) "strong, womanly"; (Old French) "song of joy." Carey, Cari, Carleen, Carlen, Carley, Carlin, Carlina, Carlita, Carlotta, Carlyn, Caro, Carole, Carolina, Carolyn, Carri, Carrie, Carroll, Carry, Cary, Caryl, Charla, Charleen, Charlena, Charlene, Charlotta, Charmain, Charmaine, Cheryl, Cherlyn, Karel, Kari, Karla, Karlen, Karleen, Karlotta, Lola, Lolita, Lotta, Lotte, Lottie, Sharleen, Sharlene, Sharline, Sharyl, Sherrie, Sherry, Sheryl.

*Caroline* (Latin) "little and womanly." Feminine form of Carl. Charles, Carla, Carlen, Carlene, Carley, Carlin, Carline, Carlita, Carlota, Carly, Carlynn, Carole, Carolin, Carolynn, Carroll, Cary, Charla, Charlena, Charlene, Karla, Karlene.

*Carrie* Familiar form of Caroline.

*Casey* (Celtic) "brave."

*Cassandra* (Greek) "helper of men; disbelieved by men." Cass, Cassi, Cassie, Cassy, Sandi, Sandy.

*Catherine* (Greek) "pure." An Anglo-Saxon form of Katherine. Caitlin, Catrin, Caren, Carin, Caron, Caryn, Cass, Cassy, Caitlaina, Catarina,

Caterina, , Catha, Catharina, Catharine, Catherina, Cathi, Cathie, Cathleen, Cathrine, Cathryn, Cathy, Cati, Caye.

*Cecilia* (Latin) "blind." Cecile, Celestine, Celia, Celie, Celina, Celinda.

*Celeste* (Latin) "heavenly." Cele, Celestine, Celia, Celina, Celinda.

*Chandra* (Sandskrit) "moon-like."

*Charity* (Latin) "benevolent; loving; charitable." Charis, Charita, Cherri, Cherry.

*Charlotte* (French) "little and womanly." A French form of Carol. Feminine form of Charles. Carla, Carlene, Carline, Carlotta, Carly, Charla, Charlene, Charmain, Cheryl, Cherlyn, Lola, Lolita, Lotta, Lotti, Lottie, Sharlene, Sherri, Sherry, Sheryl.

*Charmaine* (Latin) "little one's song." Charmain, Sharmain.

*Chastity* (Latin) "purity."

*Chelsea* (Old English) "from the ship's landing place."

*Cher* (French) "beloved." Cherie, Sher, Sherry.

*Cheryl* Familiar form of Charlotte.

*Chiquita* (Spanish) "little one."

*Chloe* (Greek) "blooming." Chloris, Cloe, Cloris.

*Christabel* (Latin-French) "beautiful Christian." Christabella, Cristabel.

*Christine* (Greek) "Christian; anointed." Chris, Chrissie, Chrissy, Christen, Christiane, Christie, Christina, Christy, Chrystal, Cris, Crissy, Cristie, Cristin, Cristine, Cristy, Crystal, Kirsten, Kirstin, Kris, Krissie, Kristen, Kristin, Kristina, Tina.

*Cicely* English form of Cecilia.

*Cindy* Short form of Cynthia.

*Claire* French form of Clara.

*Clara* (Latin) "clear; bright." Chiarra, Clair, Claire, Clare, Clarette, Clari, Clarice, Clarinda, Clarine, Clarissa, Clarita, Klara, Klarrisa.

*Clarissa* (Latin) "making famous."

*Claudia* (Latin) "lame." Feminine form of Claude. Claudette, Claudine, Gladys.

*Clementine* (Greek) "the merciful." Clemence, Clementina, Clemmie.

*Cleo* (Greek) "the famous."

*Clover* (Anglo-Saxon) "clover-blossom."

*Colette* (French-Latin) "a necklace." Collette.

*Colleen* (Celtic) "girl." Collie, Colline.

*Connie* Short form of Constance.

*Constance* (Latin) "constancy; firm of purpose." Connie, Constanta, Constantine, Costanza.

*Consuelo* (Spanish) "consolation." Consuela.

*Cora* (Greek) "maiden." Corella, Corene, Coretta, Corette, Corey, Corie, Corinna, Corinne, Corry.

*Coral* (Latin) "coral."

*Cordelia* (Welsh) "jewel of the sea." Cordi, Cordie, Cordy, Delia, Della.

*Corliss* (Teutonic) "cheerful; good-hearted."

*Cornelia* (Latin) "yellow; horn-colored." Feminine form of Cornelius. Cornela, Cornelle, Nell, Nellie.

*Courtney* (Teutonic) "from the court."
*Cyrstal* (Greek) "clear as a crystal; brilliantly pure."
*Cynthia* (Greek) "moon." Cindy.
*Cyrene* (Greek) "water nymph."

*Dagmar* (Danish) "joy of the Danes."
*Dahlia* (Scandinavian) "from the dale or valley."
*Daisy* (Anglo-Saxon) "eye of the day; flower."
*Dale* (Teutonic) "from the valley."
*Dalila* (African) "gentle." Lila.
*Dallas* (Celtic) "wise."
*Damara* (Greek) "gentle; mild." Mara, Maris.
*Damita* (Spanish) "little noble lady."
*Dana* (Scandinavian) "from Denmark." Dayna.
*Danielle* (Hebrew) "judged by God." Feminine form of Daniel. Danni, Dannie, Danny, Danya, Daniela, Danila.
*Danika* (Slavic) "the morning star." Danica.
*Daphne* (Greek) "laurel tree."
*Dara* (Hebrew) "compassion."
*Darby* (Celtic) "free man"; (Old Norse) "from the deer estate." Darb, Darbie.

*Darcie, Darcy* (Celtic) "dark."

*Daria* (Greek) "queenly." Feminine form of Darius.

*Darlene* (Anglo-Saxon) "tenderly beloved." Darla, Darline, Darrelle, Daryl.

*Daron* (Celtic) "great." Feminine form of Darren.

*Davina* (Hebrew) "beloved." Feminine form of David. Davida, Veda, Vida, Vita.

*Dawn* (Anglo-Saxon) "dawn."

*Deborah* (Hebrew) "bee." Deb, Debora, Debra, Debbi, Debbie, Debby, Devorah.

*Deirdre* (Celtic) "complete wanderer." Dee, Deidra, Didi.

*Delia* (Greek) "visible; from Delos." Dehlia, Delinda, Della.

*Delilah* (Hebrew) "pining with desire." Delila, Lila.

*Demetria* (Greek) "belonging to Demeter (godess of harvest)."

*Dena* (Hebrew) "vindicated"; (Teutonic) "from the valley." Deana, Deane. Deanna, Dina.

*Denise* (French) "adherent of Dionysus (god of wine)." Feminine form of Dennis, Denice, Denni, Dennie, Dinny.

*Desiree* (French-Latin) "desired."

*Devona* (Anglo-Saxon) "the defender."

*Diana* (Latin) "divine." Deana, Diane, Dianna, Dianne, Didi, Dyan.

*Dinah* (Hebrew) "vindicated." Dena, Dina.

*Dionne* (Greek) "divine queen." Dion, Dione, Dionis.

*Dixie* (French) "ten; tenth."

*Dolly* Greek familiar form of Dorothea.

*Dolores* (Spanish) "sorrows." Delores, Dolorita, Lola.

*Dominique* (Latin) "belonging to God." Feminine form of Dominic, Domini, Dominica.

*Donna* (Latin-Italian) "lady." Donella, Donny.

*Dora* (Greek) "gift." Dodi, Dody, Doralyn, Doralynne, Doreen, Dorena, Dorette, Dori, Dorie, Dory.

*Doris* (Greek) "of the sea." Dori, Dorice, Dorris.

*Dorothy* (Greek) "gift of God." Dasha, Dode, Dody, Dolly, Dorothea, Dorothee, Dorthea, Dottie.

*Drew* (English) "womanly one." Drue, Dru.

*Drusilla* (Greek) "dewy eyes." Dru, Drusy.

*Dulcie* (Latin) "sweetness." Delcina, Dulcea, Dulcine.

*Eartha* (Teutonic) "of the earth."

*Eda* (Anglo-Saxon) "happy; rich."

*Edana* (Celtic) "ardent or fiery."

*Eden* (Hebrew) "delightful; pleasant." Edin.

*Edith* (Teutonic) "rich gift." Eda, Ede, Edi, Edie.

*Edna* (Hebrew) "pleasure or delight." Eddi, Eddie.

*Edrea* (Teutonic) "prosperous; powerful."

*Edwina* (Anglo-Saxon) "valuable friend." Feminine form of Edwin.

*Effie* (Greek) "well spoken of."

*Eileen* Irish form of Helen.

*Eleanor* (Greek) "light." Form of Helen. Ella, Elle, Ellen, Ellie, Lena, Lenore, Nell, Nora.

*Elita* (Old French) "chosen." Elata, Lita.

*Elizabeth* (Hebrew) "oath of God." Belle, Bess, Bessie, Beth, Betsy, Bette, Bettina, Betty, Elisabeth, Elise, Elissa, Eliza, Elsa, Elsie, Elyse, Isabel, Lib, Libbie, Libby, Lisa, Lisabeth, Lise, Liz, Liza, Lusa.

*Ella* (Anglo-Saxon) "elfin." Ellette, Ellie, Elly.

*Ellen* English form of Helen. Ellyn.

*Eloise* French form of Louise.

*Elvira* (Latin) "the fair." Elva, Elvera, Elvina.

*Emily* (Teutonic-Latin) "industrious." Form of Amelia. Amelia, Ameline, Amy, Em, Emelda, Emeline, Emilie.

*Emma* (Teutonic) "ancestress." Ema, Emelinam, Ennalyn, Emmi.

*Enid* (Welsh) "purity."

*Erica* (Scandanavian) "ever-powerful, regal." Feminine form of Eric. Erika, Ricki, Rickie.

*Erin* (Celtic) "girl from Ireland." Celtic name for Ireland. Erinn, Erinna.

*Ernestine* (Teutonic) "earnest." Feminine form of Ernest. Erna, Ernaline, Ernesta.

*Estelle* (Latin) "star." Estrella, Stella.

*Esther* (Persian) "the planet Venus." Essie, Ettie, Hettie.

*Ethel* (Teutonic) "noble."

*Etta* (Teutonic) "little." Familiar form of Henrietta.

*Eudora* (Greek) "good or delightful gift." Dora, Dorrie, Eudoria.

*Eugenia* (Greek) "well-born." Feminine form of Eugene. Eugenie, Gene, Gena.

*Eunice* (Greek) "happy victory."

*Eustacia* (Latin) "fruitful; tranquil."

*Evangeline* (Greek) "bearer of glad tidings." Eva, Evangelia, Eve.

*Eve* (Hebrew) "life." Eva, Evelyn, Evie, Evita, Evonne.

*Faith* (Latin) "faithful." Fae, Fay, Faye, Fayth.

*Fallon* (Irish Gaelic) "descended from the ruler."

*Fanchon* (Teutonic) "free."

*Fanny* Familiar form of Frances. Fan, Fannie

*Fatima* (Arabic) "one who abstains." Fatma.

*Felice* (Latin) "happy." Feminine form of Felix. Felicia, Felicidad, Felicity, Felita.

*Fernanda* (Teutonic) "adventurer." Feminine form of Ferdinand. Fern.

*Fifi* (French) "one whom God will give children." Fifina, Fifine.

*Fiona* (Celtic) "fair." Finella, Fionna.

*Flavia* (Latin) "blonde, yellow-haired."

*Fleta* (Teutonic) "the fleet; swift."

*Fleur* (French-Latin) "a flower."

*Fleurette* (French) "little flower."

*Flora* (Latin) "blooming; prosperous." Flo, Flora, Florie, Florida, Florrie.

*Florence* (Latin) "flourishing."  Fiarenza, Florinda.

*Frances* (Latin) "free; from France."  Feminine form of Francis.  Fan, Fancy, Fannie, Fanny, Fran, Francesca, Franci, Francine, Francoise, Frankie, Frannie.

*Freda* (Teutonic)  "peaceful."  Short form of Frederica.  Frieda, Winifred.

*Frederica* (Teutonic)  "peaceful ruler."  Feminine form of Frederick. Freddie, Fredericka, Frederique, Rickie, Rikki.

*Freya* (Scandinavian) "honorable; noble."  Freja.

*Fulvia* (Latin) "tawny-colored."

*Gabrielle* (Hebrew) "God is my strength." Feminine form of Gabriel. Gabriella, Gabie, Gorra.

*Gail* (English) "gay; lively." Short form of Abigail. Gael, Gale, Gayle, Gayleen.

*Galina* (Russian) "of the light." Gala, Galinka.

*Genevieve* (Celtic) "white wave." Form of Guinevere. Gena, Geneva, Gennie, Gine, Jenny.

*Georgeanne* Familiar form of Georgia. Georgeanna.

*Georgia* (Greek) "husbandman." Feminine form of George. George, Georgette, Georgiana, Georgine.

*Geraldine* (Teutonic) "with a spear." Dina, Gerri, Giralda, Jeralee, Jere, Jeri, Jerry.

*Gerda* (Scandinavian) "from the protected estate." Garsha, Gerd, Gerde, Geredi.

*Germaine* (French) "German." Germain, Jermaine.

*Gertrude* (Teutonic) "spear woman." Gert, Gerty, Trudi, Trudy.

*Gianna* (Italian) "gracious one." Giannetta.

*Gilberte* (Teutonic) "illustrious pledge." Feminine form of Gilbert. Berta, Berti, Gigi, Gilberta, Gilli, Gilly.

*Gilda* (Celtic) "servant of God."

*Gillian* (Latin) "young, downy-haired child." Jill.

*Ginger* (English) "ginger-haired."

*Giselle* (Teutonic) "pledge; hostage." Gisa, Gisela.

*Gladys* (Celtic) "princess." Form of Claudia.

*Glenna* (Irish Gaelic) "from the valley or glen." Feminine form of Glenn. Glenda, Glennis, Glynnis.

*Gloria* (Latin) "glorious." Gloriana, Glory.

*Golda* (Teutonic) "gold."

*Grace* (Latin) "graceful." Gracie, Gratiana, Grayce.

*Greer* Scotch feminine form of Gregor. Grier.

*Gretchen* (German) "pearl-like." Greta, Gretel.

*Griselda* (Teutonic) "gray-haired heroine." Zelda.

*Guinevere* (Celtic) "white lady." Gennie, Gennifer, Genny, Guenevere, Gwen, Gwenore, Jen, Jennifer, Jenny, Winifred, Winnie.

*Gwendolyn* (Celtic) "white-browed." Gwen, Gwendolin, Gwennie, Gwenny, Gwyn, Gwynne, Wendi, Wendie, Wendy.

*Gwyneth* (Celtic) "blessed." Gwynne, Winnie.

*Gypsy* (English) "wanderer; rover."

*Hallie* (Greek) "thinking of the sea." Halli, Hally.

*Halona* (American Indian) "fortunate."

*Hannah* (Hebrew). "graceful." Hana, Hanni, Hannie.

*Harmony* (Latin) "harmonious one."

*Harriet* (Teutonic) "mistress of the home." Feminine form of Harry. Harriette, Hattie.

*Hayley* (Old English) "from the meadows of hay." Haley, Halie.

*Hazel* (Teutonic) "hazelnut tree." Aveline.

*Heather* (English) "flowering heather." Heath.

*Hedda* (Teutonic) "refuge in strife." Heda, Heddie, Heduika, Hedwig, Hedy.

*Heidi* (German) "of noble birth." Heida.

*Helen* (Greek) "light." Eileen, Elaine, Elana, Eleanor, Eleanore, Elena, Elenore, Ella, Elle, Ellen, Ellie, Ellyn, Helena, Helene, Ilene, Ilona, Lana, Lena, Lenore, Lenora, Lora, Nell, Nellie, Nora.

*Helga* (Scandinavian) "holy." Olga.

*Heloise* (French) Form of Eloise.

*Henrietta* (French) "Ruler of the household." Feminine form of Henry. Ettie, Hattie, Henrieta, Hettie.

*Hermione* (Greek) "of the earth." Erma, Herminia.

*Hester* (Greek) "star."

*Hilary* (Latin) "cheerful one." Hillary.

*Hilda* (Teutonic) "woman warrior." Hildy.

*Hildegarde* (Teutonic) "fortress." Hilda.

*Holly* (Old English) "holly tree." A name given to girls born near Christmas.

*Honora* (Latin) "honorable." Honey, Honor, Nora, Norah.

*Hope* (Old English) "hope."

*Hortense* (Latin) "gardener."

*Huette* (Old English) "intelligent one." Huetta.

*Hyacinth* (Greek) "beautiful youngster." Cynthia, Jacinta, Jackie.

*Iantha* (Greek) "a purple flower." Ianthina.

*Ida* (Teutonic) "happy." Idelle.

*Iesha* (Arabic) "womanly." Aisha, Ieesha.

*Ilana* (Hebrew) "big tree."

*Ilene* (English) "bright, shining one." Ileane, Iline.

*Imogene* (Latin) "image." Emogene.

*Imelda* (Old German) "battle maiden." Emelda.

*Inez* Spanish form of Agnes.

*Ingrid* (Scandinavian) "hero's daughter." Inga, Ingaberg, Inge, Inger.

*Ione* (Greek) "violet-colored stone." Iolanthe, Iola, Ionia.

*Irene* (Greek) "peace" Rena, Renee.

*Iris* (Greek) "rainbow."

*Irma* (Latin) "noble." Erma.

*Isabel* (Hebrew) "consecrated to God." Belita, Belle, Isabelle.

*Isadora* (Latin) "gift of Isis."

*Isis* (Greek) "moon goddess."

*Ivana* (Russian) Feminine form of John or Ivan.
*Ivy* (English) "ivy tree." Ivareen, Ivory.

*Jacinta* (Greek) "beautiful; comely; hyacinth flower." Giacinta, Jacinth, Jacinthe.

*Jacqueline* (Hebrew) "supplanter." Feminine form of Jacob (through Jacques) Jackelyn, Jackie, Jaclyn, Jacobina.

*Jaime* (French) "I love."

*Jamie* Feminine form of James. Jayme, Jamelle.

*Jane* (Hebrew) "God's gracious gift." Feminine form of John. Gene, Gianina, Giovanna, Jan, Janelle, Janet, Janette, Janice, Janie, Janina, Janine, Janis, Janith, Jayne, Jean, Jeanette, Jeanne, Jenny, Jessie, Jo Ann, Jo-Ann, Joan, Joanna, Joanne, Johanna, Joni, Jonie, Juanita, Shena.

*Jasmine* (Persian) "jasmine flower."

*Jean* (Old French) "gracious one." Sine.

*Jemima* (Hebrew) "dove." Jemma, Yomina.

*Jena* (Arabic) "a small bird." Jenna.

*Jennifer* (Celtic) "white; fair." Form of Guinevere. Gennie, Jen, Jennie,

Jenny.

*Jessica* (Hebrew) "wealthy." Jessalyn, Jessie.

*Jill* Familiar form of Julia. Jillian, Jilly.

*Joan* (Hebrew) "God's gracious gift." Feminine form of John. Jody, Joni.

*Jocelyn* (Latin) "playful one." Joyce, Justine.

*Joelle* (Hebrew) "the Lord is willing." Feminine form of Joel. Joelyn.

*Jolie* (French) "pretty one."

*Josephine* (Hebrew) "he shall increase." Feminine form of Joseph. Jo, Joline, Josie, Josephina, Jossette, Fifi, Fina.

*Joy* (Latin) "joy." Joi, Joyann, Joye.

*Joyce* (Latin) "joyous."

*Jaunita* (Spanish) Form of Jane. Jauna.

*Judith* (Hebrew) "of Judah." Jody, Judi, Judy.

*Julia* (Latin) "youthful." Feminine form of Julius. Giulia, Juliana, Juliana, Julie, Juliet, Juliette.

*June* (Latin) "June." Junette, Junia.

*Justine* (Latin) "just." Feminine form of Justin.

*Kai* (Scandinavian) "henlike." Kay, Ky, Kyle, Kylie.

*Kalika* (Greek) "rosebud." Kallie.

*Kalila* (Arabic) "beloved." Kalie, Kallet.

*Kalinda* (Sandskrit) "sun."

*Kama* (Sandskrit) "love." Mythological: the Hindu god of love.

*Kara* (Greek) "pure." Cara, Karalee, Karrah.

*Karen* Danish form of Katherine. Caren, Kari, Karin.

*Katherine* (Greek) "pure." Caitlin, Caitrin, Caren, Caron, Cass, Cassie, Cassy, Catlaina, Catarina, Catha, Cathe, Catherine, Cathryn, Cathy, Catie, Caty, Caye, Karen, Karena, Kari, Karin, Kassi, Kate, Katerina, Katerine, Katey, Katha, Kathie, Kathleen, Kathryn, Kathy, Katie, Katina, Katrinka, Katti, Kay, Kaye, Kit, Kitty.

*Kayley* (Irish Gaelic) "descendent of the slender one." Kaleigh.

*Keely* (Celtic) "beautiful." Keelin, Kiley.

*Kelly* (Gaelic) "warrior woman."

*Kelsey* (Old Norse) "from the ship-island."

*Kenda* (Old English) knowing one from the hills." Kenna, Kinna.

*Kerry* (Irish Gaelic) "dark; dark-haired."

*Kimberly* (Teutonic) "from the royal fortress meadow." Kim

*Kirsten* Danish form of Christine. Curstag, Kirsten, Krista, Kristel, Kristi, Kristin.

*Kyra* (Greek) "lordly one." Kiri, Kyran.

*Lacey* (French) "a young lady."  Lacie, Lacy.
*Lainey* Familiar form of Elaine.
*Lana* (English) Form Helen.  Lanna, Lanny.
*Lane* (Middle English) "from the narrow road."  Lanie, Lanni.
*Lani* (Hawaiian) "sky."
*Lara* (Latin) "famous."
*Larissa* (Latin) "cheerful."  Lacey, Lissa.
*Latisha* (Latin) "happy one."  Letetia, Latasha.
*Laura* (Latin) "crown of laurel."  Feminine form of Lawrence.  Laure,
    Laureen, Laurel, Lauren, Laurette, Lora, Loreen, Loren, Lorena,
    Lorene, Lorette, Lorette, Lori, Lorinda, Lorna.
*Laverne* (French) "springlike."  Laverna, La Verne, Verna.
*Lavinia* (Latin) "purified."  Levana, Vinni.
*Leah* (Hebrew) "weary."  Lea, Lee, Leigh.
*Leandre* (Greek) "like a lioness."  Leanda, Leodora.
*Lee* (Gaelic) "poetic"; (English) "from the pasture."  Leean, Leanna.

*Leila* (Arabic) "dark as night." Lela, Lelah, Lelia.

*Leona* (Latin) "lion." Feminine form of Leo.

*Leontine* (Latin) "lionlike." Leontyne.

*Leslie* (Celtic) "from the gray fort." Lesley, Lezlie.

*Letitia* (Latin) "joy." Leta, Letice, Letty, Tish.

*Levana* (Latin) "of the dawn."

*Lida* (Slavic) "beloved of the people."

*Lila* Short form of Dalila. Delilah, Lillian.

*Lillian* (Latin) "lily flower." Lila.

*Linda* (Spanish) "pretty." Lyndie, Lynda.

*Lindsay, Lindsey* (Teutonic) "from the linden tree island." Linsay, Linsey.

*Linette* (Celtic) "graceful"; (French) "linnet (bird)."

*Lisa* (English) "allied with God." Leesa, Lisetta, Liza.

*Lona* (Middle English) "solitary." Loni.

*Lorelei* (German) "alluring." Lorilee, Lurleen.

*Loretta* (English) Form of Laura.

*Lorraine* (French) "from Lorraine." Laraine, Lori.

*Lotus* (Greek) "lotus flower."

*Louise* (Teutonic) "famous woman warrior." Feminine form of Louis. Allison, Aloisia, Aloysia, Eloisa, Eloise, Lois, Lola, Lolita, Lou, Lu, Lulu.

*Luana* (Old German-Hebrew) "graceful woman warrior."

*Lucy* (Latin) "light." Feminine form of Lucius; Luke. Lucia, Luciana, Lucie, Lucille, Lucinda.

*Ludmilla* (Old Slavic) "loved by the people."

*Luella* (Old English) "elf." Louella, Lulu.

*Luna* (Latin) "shining."

*Lydia* (Greek) "from Lydia."

*Lynette* Familiar form of Linette; Lynn.

*Lynn* (Anglo-Saxon) "a cascade, or light pool below a fall." Linn, Lynne.

*Mabel* (Latin) "lovable."

*Madeline* (Hebrew) "the tower." Lena, Lynn, Madalyn, Madelaine, Madeleine, Madge, Magdalene, Marlene, Maude.

*Mahalia* (Hebrew) "affection."

*Maida* (Anglo-Saxon) "maiden."

*Mallory* (Old German) "war counselor." Malorie, Malory.

*Mara* Hebrew form of Mary.

*Marcella* (Latin) "belonging to Mars." Marcy.

*Marcia* (Latin) "warlike." Marcie, Marsha.

*Margaret* (Greek) "pearl." Gretchen, Gretel, Madge, Maggie, Margarette, Margarita, Marge, Margie, Margo, Marguerite, Marjorie, Marjory, Meg, Megan, Meghan, Peg, Peggy, Rita.

*Marian* Combination of Mary and Ann. Mariam, Marianne, Marion, Maryann.

*Marina* (Latin) "maid of the sea."

*Martha* (Arabic) "lady." Marta, Marti, Martie, Martina, Mattie, Pat,

Patti, Patty.

*Mary* (Hebrew) "bitter." Commemorating the Virgin Mary, now the most frequently bestowed name in all Christian countries. Its true meaning, long since discarded or lost, is "bitter," a Hebrew word with biblical significance. Mame, Mamie, Mara, Maria, Mariae, Marian, Marianne, Marie, Marilee, Marilyn, Larin, Marion, Marlo, Maryann, Marysa, Maura, Maureen, Mavra, Meridel, Mimi, Minnie, Miriam, Mitzi, Moira, Molly, Muriel.

*Matilda* (Teutonic) "mighty." Matty, Maude.

*Maureen* (Latin) "dark." Irish familiar form of Mary. Maura, Maurene.

*Mavis* (Celtic) "thrush."

*Maxine* (Latin) "greatest." Feminine form of Max. Maxene, Maxi.

*May* (Latin) "great"; (Anglo-Saxon) "kinswoman." Mae, Maya, Maye.

*Meade* (Greek) "honey wine."

*Meara* (Irish Gaelic) "mirth."

*Megan* (Anglo-Saxon) "strong or able." Meg, Meghan.

*Melanie* (Greek) "dark-clothed." Mela, Melantha, Melonie, Milena.

*Melba* (Greek) "soft; slender."

*Melina* (Latin) "canary-colored."

*Melinda* (Greek) "dark; gentle." Linda, Lindy, Malinda, Mandy.

*Melissa* (Greek) "honey bee." Lissa, Milicent, Millie, Missie.

*Melody* (Greek) "song." Melodie.

*Meredith* (Welsh) "guardian from the sea." Meridith, Merry.

*Merle* (Latin) "blackbird."

*Mia* (Italian) "mine; my."

*Michelle* (Hebrew) " who is like the Lord?" Feminine form of Michael. Micky, Midge.

*Mildred* (Anglo-Saxon) "gentle counselor." Millie.

*Millicent* (Teutonic) "strength." Mel, Milicent, Milly, Missy.

*Mindy* Familiar form of Melinda; Minna. Minette.

*Minerva* (Greek) "wisdom."

*Minnie* Familiar form of Minerva; Wilhelmina.

*Mirabel* (Latin) "extraordinary beauty." Mira, Mirabella, Mirka, Myra.

*Miranda* (Latin) "admirable." Mandy, Mira, Myro, Randy.

*Miriam* Original Hebrew form of Mary. Mimi, Mitzi.

*Mona* (Greek) "solitary"; (Irish Gaelic) "noble." Moyna.

*Monica* (Latin) "advisor." Monique.

*Morgan* (Old Welsh) "from the seashore." Morgana, Morganne, Morgen.

*Morna* (Celtic) "gentle."

*Muriel* (Arabic) "myrrh"; (Irish Gaelic) "sea-bright."

*Myrtle* (Greek) "a shrub or tree."

*Nadine* (French-Slavic) "hope." Nadia, Nady, Nadzia, Natka.

*Nan* Familiar form of Ann. Nana, Nancy, Nanette, Nettie.

*Naomi* (Hebrew) "pleasant." Naoma, Naomia.

*Natalie* (Latin) "Christmas child." Natala, Nataline, Nathalia, Natividad, Talya.

*Natasha* Russian familiar form of Natalie. Tasha.

*Neala* (Celtic) "chieftainess."

*Neda* (Slovakian) "born on a Sunday." Nedi.

*Nerissa* (Greek) "of the sea."

*Nerys* (Modern Welsh) "lordly one."

*Nicole* (Greek) "victory of the people." Colette, Cosette, Nicki, Nicola, Nikki.

*Nina* (Hebrew) "grace"; (Spanish) "little girl." Nena, Ninetta, Ninette, Nino.

*Noel* (Latin-French) "Christmas; born of Christmas day." Noelle, Noella, Noellyn.

*Nola* (Celtic) "noble; famous."  Nolana, Noleen.
*Norma* (Latin) "rule; pattern."  Noreen, Noria, Norina, Normia.
*Nova* (Latin) "new one."
*Nydia* (Latin) "from the nest."
*Nyssa* (Greek) "beginning."  Nissa.

*Octavia* (Latin) "eighth." Feminine form of Octavius. Octavie, Ottavia, Tavia, Tavie.

*Odelia* (Teutonic) "wealthy." Odette, Odilia, Othelia, Uta.

*Odessa* (Greek) "from the long journey."

*Olga* (Teutonic) "holy." Helga, Olenka, Olna, Olva.

*Olivia* (Latin) "olive tree." Liva, Livia, Nola, Nolita, Olive.

*Olympia* (Greek) "heavenly one." Olympe.

*Opal* (Hindu) "precious stone." Opalina, Opaline.

*Ophelia* (Greek) "immortality and wisdom." Felia, Ophelie, Phelia.

*Oprah* (Hebrew) "fawnlike." Ofra, Ophrah.

*Oriana* (Latin) "golden." Oriane.

*Oriole* (Latin) "fair-haired." Oralie, Oriel.

*Orla* (Irish Gaelic) "golden lady." Orlagh.

*Ornella* (Italian) "from the flowering ash trees." Ornetta.

*Paige* (Teutonic) "child." Page.

*Pamela* (Greek) "all-honey." Pam, Pammy.

*Pandora* (Greek) "all-gifted." Doria.

*Patience* (Latin) "one who endures suffering."

*Patricia* (Latin) "of the nobility." Feminine form of Patrick. Pat, Patrice, Patsy, Patty, Tricia, Trish.

*Paula* (Latin) "little." Feminine form of Paul. Paulette, Pauline, Polly.

*Pearl* (Latin) "pearl." Perle, Perry.

*Penelope* (Greek) "weaver." Penny.

*Petra* (Greek) "stonelike." Peta.

*Petrina* (Latin) "rock." Feminine form of Peter. Pier, Perrine.

*Petula* (Latin) "seeker."

*Philippa* (Greek) "lover of horses." Feminine form of Phillip.

*Philomena* (Greek) "well-loved." Filomena, Mena.

*Phoebe* (Greek) "shining." Phebe.

*Phyllis* (Greek) "green bough." Phillis, Phyllida.

*Pilar* (Spanish) "foundation."  Pili, Pilita.
*Portia* (Latin) "offering."  Tia.
*Prima* (Latin) "firstborn."
*Priscilla* (Latin) "from ancient times."  Ciulla, Prissy.
*Prudence* (Latin) "foresight; intelligence."  Pru, Pruddie.

*Queenie* (Old English) "queenlike."
*Querida* (Spanish) "loved one."
*Quiana* (Native American) "graceful."
*Quinta* (Latin) "five; fifth child." Feminine form of Quentin.
*Quintessa* (Latin) "the essense." Tessa.

*Rachel* (Hebrew) "ewe." Rae, Racquel, Rochelle, Shelly.

*Ramona* (Teutonic) "mighty of wise protectress." Feminine form of Raymond.

*Randy* Short form of Randall.

*Rani* (Sandskrit) "queen." Rana.

*Raphaela* (Hebrew) "healer." Rafa.

*Rebecca* (Hebrew) "the ensnarer." Becky, Reba, Riva.

*Regina* (Latin) "queen." Regan, Reggi, Reina, Rina.

*Remy* (French) "one from Rheims."

*Rena* (Hebrew) "song."

*Renata* (Latin) "reborn."

*Rhea* (Greek) "mother of the gods." Rea, Rhya, Ria.

*Rhoda* (Greek) "a rose." Rhodie, Roda, Rodi, Rodina.

*Rhonda* ( Scottish Gaelic) "strong one." Rona.

*Risa* (Latin) "laughter."

*Roberta* (Teutonic) "shining with fame." Feminine form of Robert.
Bobbie, Robbie.

*Robin* (Teutonic) "robin." Familiar form of Roberta. Robbie, Robina.

*Rochelle* (French) "from the little rock." Form of Rachel. Shelly.

*Rona* (Teutonic) "mighty power." Feminie form of Ronald. Rhona.

*Rosalie* (Irish) Familiar form of Rose. Rosaleen.

*Rosalind* (Spanish) "beautiful rose." Ros, Rosalinda, Rosalyn, Roz.

*Rosamond* (Teutonic) "famous protector."

*Rose* (Latin) "rose." Rhoda, Rosaleen, Rose, Rosalie, Rosella, Rosetta,
Rosie, Zita.

*Rosemary* (Latin) "dew of the sea." Rosemarie.

*Rowena* (Celtic) "white mane." Rena, Ronnie.

*Roxane* (Persian) "dawn of the day." Roxanna, Roxanne.

*Ruby* (Latin) "ruby."

*Ruth* (Hebrew) "friend of beauty." Ruthie.

*Sabina* (Latin) "Sabine woman." Bina, Sabu, Sabine, Savina.
*Sabrina* (Latin) "legendary English princess." Brina, Zabrina.
*Sacha* (Greek) "helper of mankind."
*Salome* (Hebrew) "peaceful."
*Samantha* (Aramaic) "listener." Samella, Samelle, Samuella, Samuelle.
*Samara* (Hebrew) "from ancient city of Samaria.
*Sandra* (Greek) "helper of mankind." Saundra, Zandra.
*Sapphire* (Greek) "sapphire stone; sapphire blue."
*Sarah* (Hebrew) "princess." Sadie, Sal, Sallt, Sara, Sari, Shara, Shari,
    Sharon, Sheree, Sherri, Sorcha, Zara.
*Sasha* (Russian) Form of Alexander. Sacha.
*Selena* (Greek) "moon." Selene, Salina.
*Selma* (Celtic) "fair." Zelma.
*Seraphina* (Hebrew) "burning; ardent." Serafina, Seraphine.
*Serena* (Latin) "calm; tranquil." Rena, Serenna, Serina.
*Shaina* (Hebrew) "beautiful." Shaine, Shane, Shayna.

*Shani* (African) "marvelous."

*Shannon* (Irish Gaelic) "old; wise." Shane, Shanna, Shauna, Shawna.

*Sharon* (Hebrew) "from the open plain." Shara, Shari, Sharona, Sharyn, Sherri.

*Sheba* (Hebrew) "from the Sheba."

*Sheena* Irish from Jane. Shena.

*Sheila* Irish form of Cecilia. Sheela, Sheilah, Shell

*Shirley* (Old English) "from the white meadow." Sherill, Sher, Sherri, Sherrie, Sherry

*Sibyl* (Greek) "prophetess." Cybil, Sibby, Sybil.

*Sigourney* (Scandinavian) "victorious." Signi, Signy.

*Simone* (Hebrew) "one who hears." Feminine form of Simon. Simonette.

*Sophie* (Greek) "wisdom." Sofia, Sofie, Sonia, Sonja, Sonny, Sonya, Sophia.

*Stella* (Latin) "star."

*Stephanie* (Greek) "garland." Feminine form of Stephen. Stephani, Stesha, Stevana.

*Summer* (Old English) "summer."

*Susan* (Hebrew) "lily." Sue, Suki, Susanna, Susannah, Susanne, Susie, Suzan, Suzanna, Suzanne, Suzie, Suzy.

*Sydney* (Old French) "from the city of St. Denis." Syd, Sydel, Sydelle.

*Sylvia* (Latin) "forest maiden." Silvia, Silvie, Sylvanna, Zilvia.

*Tabitha* (Aramaic) "gazelle." Tabbi, Tabby, Tabita.

*Taffy* (Old Welsh) "beloved."

*Talia* (Greek) "blooming." Taletha, Talicia, Talita.

*Tallulah* (Choctaw Indian) "leaping water." Tallie, Tallou, Talula.

*Tamara* (Hebrew) "palm tree." Tammi, Tammy, Tamour, Tamra.

*Tammy* (Hebrew) "perfection."

*Tanya* (Russian) "fairy queen." Tania, Tanja, Tati.

*Tara* (Irish Gaelic) "tower." Tarah.

*Tatiana* (Russian) "fairy queen."

*Teresa* (Greek) "the harvester." Tera, Terse, Teri, Terri, Terry.

*Tessa* (Greek) "fourth." Tess, Tessie.

*Thalassa* (Greek) "she who comes from the sea."

*Thalia* (Greek) "joyful; blooming."

*Thea* (Greek) "divine."

*Thelma* (Greek) "nursling."

*Theodora* (Greek) "divine gift." Teddie, Theda, Theodosia, Theodora.

*Thirza* (Hebrew) "pleasant one."

*Theresa* (Greek) "reaper." Tera, Teresa, Terese, Teri, Terri, Terrie, Terry, Tess, Tessy, Therese, Tracy.

*Thomasina* (Greek) "little twin." Feminine form of Thomas. Tammi, Tammie, Thomasa, Tommie.

*Thora* (Teutonic) "thunder." Feminine form of Thor. Tyra.

*Tiara* (Greek) "with a jeweled headress." Tia, Tiana.

*Tiffany* (Greek) "appearance of God." Tiff, Tiffani, Tiffy.

*Timothea* (Greek) "honoring God." Feminine form of Timothy. Tim, Timmi, Timmy.

*Titania* (Greek) "giant." Tania.

*Toby* (Hebrew) "God is good." Feminine form of Tobias. Toby.

*Toni* (Latin) "special beyond price." Short form of Antonia.

*Tracy* (Latin) "courageous." Tracey, Tracie.

*Trina* (Greek) "pure one." Treena.

*Trista* (Latin) "the sorrowful."

*Trixie* (Latin) "bearer of joy." Form of Beatrix.

*Tuesday* (English) "Tuesday."

*Twyla* (English) "abbreviation of twighlight."

*Tyre* (Old English) "river."

*Udele* (Anglo-Saxon) "rich; prosperous; ruler of all." Uda, Udo.

*Ulrika* (Old German) "one with large estate."

*Uma* (Latin) "one," Irish form of Agnes. Ona, Oona.

*Undine* (Latin) "from the waves."

*Unity* (English) "unity."

*Uriel* (Hebrew) "light of God." Urice.

*Ursula* (Latin) "little bear." Ursa, Ursulina, Ursuline.

*Valda* (Scandinavian) "renowned ruler." Valdis, Velda.
*Valentina* (Latin) "strong; valiant." Val, Valencia, Valentine, Tina.
*Valerie* (Latin) "strong." Val, Valaree, Valeska, Valetta, Valia
*Valonia* (Latin) "from the vale."
*Vanessa* (Greek) "butterfly." Esther, Nessi, Van, Vanna, Vanni.
*Venus* (Latin) "Venus (goddess of beauty)." Venitia.
*Vera* (Latin) "true"; (Russian) "faith." Verena.
*Verna* (Latin) "sringlike." Vern, Vernis.
*Verona* (Italian) "one from Verona."
*Veronica* (Latin-Greek) "true image." Form of Bernice. Rossi, Ronnir,
    Vera, Veronika, Veronique, Vonni.
*Vesta* (Latin) "one who guards the fire."
*Victoria* (Latin) "the victorious." Feminine form of Victor. Vicki,
    Vicky, Vikki.
*Vina* (Spanish) "of the vineyard."
*Violet* (Latin) "violet flower." Lolande, Lolanthe, Vi, Viola, Violette,

Yolande.

*Virginia* (Latin) "virginal; maidenly."  Ginger, Ginny, Jinny, Virgie.

*Vita* (Hebrew) "beloved one."  Veda, Vitia.

*Vivian* (Latin) "lively."  Viv, Vivianne, Vivien.

*Voleta* (Old French) "with a flowering veil."  Voletta.

*Wallis* (Teutonic) "from Wales." Feminine form of Wallace.

*Wanda* (Teutonic) "wanderer." Wendi, Wendy.

*Wanetta* (Old English) "pale one." Wynetta.

*Wesley* (Old English) "from the west meadow." Leigh, Wellesley.

*Whitney* (Old English) "from the white island."

*Willow* (English) "thin and graceful."

*Wilhelmina* (Teutonic) "resolute guardian." Feminine form of
William. Billi, Billie, Min, Minnie, Velma, Vilma, Willa, Willamina,
Willie, Wilma, Wilmette

*Wilona* (Old English) "desired."

*Winnifred* (Teutonic) "friend of peace." Freddi, Freddie, Oona, Una,
Winnie.

*Wynne* (Celtic) "fair." Short form of Gwendolyn.

*Wynona* (Native American) "firstborn girl." Wenonah, Winona.

*Xanthe* (Greek) "yellow-haired."

*Xaviera* (Arabic) "brilliant." Feminine form of Xavier.

*Xenia* (Greek) "hospitable." Xena, Zena, Zina.

*Xylona* (Greek) "one from the forest." Xylene, Xylia.

*Yaffa* (Hebrew) "beautiful one."
*Yasmine* (Arabic) "like the jasmine flower."
*Yelena* (Russian) "of the light."
*Yente* (Hebrew) "kind one."
*Yolanda* French form of Violet.  Yolande.
*Yseult* (Welsh) "fair one."  Ysanne, Ysolde.
*Yvonne* (Old French) "archer."  Feminine form of Ivar.  Ives, Yvette.

*Zahava* (Modern Hebrew) "golden one."

*Zara* (Hebrew) "dawn." Form of Sarah. Zara, Zaria.

*Zelda* (Old German) "battle maiden." Zelde.

*Zita* Short form of names ending in "sita" or "zita."

*Zoe* (Greek) "life."

*Zofia* (Polish) "wise one." Zifuam, Zosia.

*Zona* (Greek) "girdlelike."

*Zora* (Slavic) "aurora."

*Zsa Zsa* Hungarian form of Susan.

*Zula* (English) "from the Zulu people."

# Chapter 7

# Boy's Names

*Aaron* (Hebrew) "exalted one." Aaren, Ari, Arnie, Aron, Erin, Haroun.

*Abbot* (Hebrew) "father; abbot." Abbie.

*Abdul* (Arabic) " son of." The name may be used with another name or independently.

*Abel* (Hebrew) "breath." Abe.

*Abner* (Hebrew) "father of light."

*Abraham* (Hebrew) "father of the multitude."

*Abram* (Hebrew) "exalted father."

*Adair* (Celtic) "from the oak tree ford."

*Adam* (Hebrew) "man of the red earth."

*Addison* (Old English) "son of Adam."

*Adlai* (Hebrew) "my witness."

*Adler* (Teutonic) "eagle."

*Adolph* (Teutonic) "noble wolf." Dolf.

*Adrian* (Latin) "from Adria, Italy." Adrien, Hadrian.

*Alan* (Celtic) "handsome; fair." Alain, Allan, Allen, Allie, Allyn.

*Alastair* Scotch form of Alexander.

*Alben* (Latin) "fair; blond."

*Albert* (Teutonic) "noble and brilliant." Adelbert, Al, Albrecht, Bert.

*Alden* (Old English) "old, wise protector."

*Aldous* (Old German) "from the old house."

*Aldrich* (Old English) "old wise ruler." Aldridge, Eldridge, Rich.

*Alexander* "helper of mankind." Alastair, Al, Alec, Alex, Alexandre, Sandy.

*Alfred* (Teutonic) "elf counselor." Al, Avery Fred.

*Alger* (Anglo-Saxon) "noble spearman." Short form of Algernon.

*Algernon* (Old French) "bearded."

*Ali* (Arabic) "greatness."

*Allard* (Teutonic) "noble; resolute."

*Aloysius* (Teutonic) "famous in war."

*Alphonse* (Teutonic) "eager for battle." Alonzo, Alphonso, Fons.

*Alvin* (Teutonic) "beloved by all."

*Ambrose* (Greek) "immortal."

*Amory* (Teutonic) "industrious."

*Amos* (Hebrew) "burden."

*Anatole* (Greek) "man from the east."

*Andrew* (Greek) "manly." Anders Andre, Andy, Drew.

*Angus* (Celtic) "exceptionally strong." Ennis, Gus.

*Ansel* (Teutonic) "divine protector."

*Anson* (Anglo-Saxon) "son of Ann."

*Anthony* (Latin) "priceless." Antone, Antonio, Tony.

*Apollo* (Greek) "manly."

*Archer* (Latin) "bowman."

*Archibald* (Teutonic) "bold."

*Arden* (Latin) "ardent; fervent."

*Arlen* (Celtic) "pledge."

*Armand* (Teutonic) "warrior." Armin.

*Armstrong* (Old English) "strong arm."

*Arnold* (Teutonic) "mighty as an eagle."

*Artemus* (Greek) "gift of Artemis."

*Arthur* (Welsh) "brave."

*Arvad* (Hebrew) "wanderer."

*Arvin* (Teutonic) "friend of the people.

*Asa* (Hebrew) "physician."

*Asher* (Hebrew) "happy."

*Ashley* (Teutonic) "from the ash tree meadow."

*Athol* (Scottish-Gaelic) "from Ireland."

*Aubrey* (Teutonic) "ruler of the elves."

*August* (Latin) "majestic dignity." Historical: the name honors
    Augustus Caesar. Austin.

*Augustine* (Latin) "belonging to Augustus." Agustin.

*Averill* (Anglo-Saxon) "born in April." Ave, Averil.

*Avery* English form of Alfred.

*Axel* (Scandinavian) "father of peace."  Form of the Hebrew name Absalom.

*Bailey* (French) "bailiff; steward."

*Baird* (Celtic) "ballad singer." Barr.

*Baldwin* (Teutonic) "bold friend."

*Bancroft* (Old English) "from the bean field." Ban, Bank, Bink.

*Barclay* (Old English) "from the birch tree meadow." Bar, Berk, Berkley.

*Barlow* (Old English) "from the bare hill."

*Barnabas* (Hebrew) "son of prophecy." Barnaby, Barney.

*Barnes* (Old English) "bear-like."

*Barnett* (Teutonic) "bear-like." Barry.

*Baron* (Teutonic) "noble warrior."

*Barry* (Old English) "one living near the berries."

*Bartco* (Old English) "from the barley farm."

*Bartholomew* (Hebrew) "son of the ploughman." Bart, Barth, Barthelemy, Bartlett, Bartolome.

*Basil* (Greek) "kingly." Basile, Vassily.

*Baxter* (Old English) "baker."

*Bayard* (Teutonic) "having red-brown hair." Bay.

*Beauregard* (Old English) "handsome." Beau, Bo.

*Benedict* (Latin) "blessed." Ben, Benedetto, Benito, Benny.

*Benjamin* (Hebrew) "son of the right hand." Ben, Benji, Bennie, Jamie.

*Bennett* (French) "blessed, small one." Benet.

*Benson* (Hebrew) "son of Benjamin."

*Benton* (Old Englsih) "of the moors." Bent.

*Bergen* (Scandinavian) "from the mountain."

*Berkeley* Form of Barclay. Berk, Berkly.

*Bernard* (Teutonic) "brave bear." Barnard, Barney, Bern, Bernardo, Bernhard, Bernie, Berny, Bjorn.

*Bert* (Teutonic) "bright." Burt.

*Bertram* (Teutonic) "glorious raven." Bart, Bertrand.

*Bevan* (Celtic) "son of Evan." Bevin.

*Bjorn* Scandinavian form of Bern.

*Blaine* (Celtic) "thin; lean." Blane, Blayne.

*Blair* (Celtic) "from the plain."

*Blake* (Old English) "fair-haired and fair-complected."

*Blaze* (Latin) "stammerer."

*Bogart* (Old French) "strong as a bow." Bo, Bogie.

*Bond* (Teutonic) "tiller of the soil."

*Boone* (Old English) "good." Bone, Boonie, Boony.

*Booth* (Teutonic) "from the market stall."  Boothe, Boot.

*Borden* (Anglo-Saxon) "from the valley of the boar."

*Boris* (Slavic) "warrior."

*Bowden* (Celtic) "yellow-haired."  Bowen, Boyd.

*Boyce* (Teutonic) "woodland dweller."

*Brad* (Old English) "broad."

*Braden* (Old English) "from the wide valley."

*Bradford* (Old English) "from the broad river crossing."  Brad, Ford.

*Bradley* (Old English) "from the broad meadow."  Brad, Lee, Leigh.

*Bram* (Irish Gaelic) "raven"; (Old English) "fierce; famous."

*Brandon* (Teutonic) "from the beacon hill."  Bran, Brand, Brandy.

*Brendan* (Celtic) "little raven."  Bren, Brenden, Brendin, Brendon.

*Brent* (Old English) "steep hill."

*Bret, Brett* (Celtic) "a Briton, or native of Brittany."  Britt.

*Brewster* (Old English) "brewer."  Brew, Brewer, Bruce.

*Brian* (Celtic) "strength; virtue."  Briant, Brien, Brion, Bryan, Bryant, Bryon.

*Brigham* (Old English) "from the enclosed bridge."  Brig.

*Brock* (Old English) "badger."

*Broderick* (Welsh) "son of Roderick."  Brod, Rick, Ricky.

*Bronson* (Old English) son of the dark-skinned one."  Bron, Sonny.

*Brooks* (Old English) "from the brook."

*Bruce* (Old French) "from the brushwood thicket."

*Bruno* (Teutonic) "brown-haired."

*Bud* (Old English) "messenger." Budd, Buddy.

*Burgess* (Teutonic) "citizen of a fortified town." Burr.

*Burke* (Teutonic) "from the fortress." Bourke, Burk.

*Burl* (Old English) "cupbearer." Burlie.

*Burne* (Teutonic) "from the brook." Bourn, Bourne, Burn, Byrne.

*Burton* (Teutonic) "from the fortress."

*Byrd* (Old English) "birdlike."

*Byron* (Teutonic) "from the cottage." Biron.

*Cadell* (Celtic) "with a marital spirit."

*Caesar* (Latin) "long-haired."

*Calder* (Celtic) "stream." Cal.

*Caldwell* (Teutonic) "cold spring." Cal.

*Caleb* (Hebrew) "faithful." Cale.

*Calvert* (Old English) "herdsman."

*Calvin* (Latin) "bald." Cal, Vin, Vinnie.

*Cameron* (Scottish Gaelic) "crooked nose." Cam.

*Campbell* (Scottish Gaelic) "crooked mouth." Cam, Campy.

*Canute* (Old Norse) "knot." Knute.

*Carey* (Old Welsh) "from the fortress." Cary.

*Carleton* (Old English) "from Carl's farm." Carl, Carlton, Charlton.

*Carlin* (Celtic) "little champion." Carl, Carlie, Carly.

*Carlisle* (Old English) "from the walled city." Carlyle.

*Carlos* Spanish form of Charles.

*Carmine* (Latin) "song."

*Carney* (Celtic) "warrior." Car, Carny, Kearney.

*Carroll* (Celtic) "champion." Familiar form of Charles. Carrol, Cary, Caryl.

*Carson* (Old English) "son of the family on the marsh."

*Carter* (Old English) "car driver."

*Carver* (Old English) "wood carver."

*Casey* (Celtic) "brave."

*Casper* (Persian) "treasurer." Cass, Gaspar, Gasparo, Jasper.

*Cassidy* (Celtic) "clever."

*Cassius* (Latin) "vain."

*Cato* (Latin) "keen; wise."

*Cecil* (Latin) "blind."

*Cedric* (Celtic) "chieftain." Rick.

*Chad* (Old English) "warlike." Short form of Chadwick, Chadbourne. Familiar form of Charles.

*Chaim* (Hebrew) "life." Hy, Hyman, Hymie, Manny.

*Chalmers* (Teutonic) "lord of the household."

*Chandler* (Old French) "candlemaker."

*Channing* (Old English) "knowing"; (Old French) "cannon." Chan.

*Chapman* (Anglo-Saxon) "merchant." Chappie, Mannie.

*Charles* (Teutonic) "manly; strong." Carl, Carlo, Carlos, Carrol, Carroll, Cary, Caryl, Chad, Charley, Charlie, Chick, Chuck, Karl.

*Chase* (Old French) "hunter."

*Chauncey* (Latin) "chancellor; church official." Chance.

*Chen* (Chinese) "great."

*Chester* (Old English) "from the fortified town." Short form of Rochester. Ches, Chet.

*Chilton* (Old English) "from the farm by the spring."

*Christian* (Greek) "follower of Christ." Chris, Christiano, Kit, Krispin, Kris, Kristian.

*Christopher* (Greek) "Christ-bearer." Chris, Christoph, Crit, Kit, Kristo.

*Cian* (Irish Gaelic) "ancient one." Keane.

*Clarence* (Latin) "bright; famous." Clare, Clair.

*Clark* (Old French) "scholar."

*Claude* (Latin) "lame."

*Clayborne* (Teutonic) "born of the earth; mortal." Claiborn, Clay, Clayborn, Claybourne.

*Clayton* (Old English) "from the town built on the clay bed."

*Clement* (Latin) "merciful." Clem, Clemens, Clemente, Klement.

*Cleveland* (Old English) "from the cliffs." Cleve.

*Clifford* (Old English) "from the cliff at the river crossing." Cliff.

*Clifton* (Old English) "steep rock; cliff." Short form of Clifford.

*Clinton* (Teutonic) "from the headland farm." Clint.

*Clive* (Old English) "cliff dweller."

*Clyde* (Welsh) "heard from afar."

*Colbert* (Old English) "outstanding seafarer." Cole.

*Colby* (Old English) "from the black farm." Cole.

*Coleman* (Irish) "dove."

*Colin* (Irish Gaelic) "child." Colan, Collin.

*Collier* (Old English) "miner."

*Conan* (Celtic) "wise." Con, Conant, Connie.

*Conlan* (Anglo-Saxon) "hero." Connie.

*Conrad* (Teutonic) "able counselor." Con, Connie, Cort, Konrad, Kurt.

*Conroy* (Irish) "wise man." Roy.

*Constantine* (Latin) "firm; constant." Constantin, Costa.

*Conway* (Celtic) "hound of the plain."

*Cooper* (Old English) "barrel maker."

*Corbin* (Latin) "raven." Corbett, Corby, Cory.

*Cordell* (French) "ropemaker." Cord, Cordie, Cory.

*Corey* (Irish Gaelic) "from the round hill." Cory.

*Cornelius* (Latin) "war horn." Connie, Cornell, Nell.

*Cosmo* (Greek) "well-ordered." Cos.

*Courtland* (Anglo-French) "from the farmstead or court land." Court.

*Craig* (Scottish) "from near the crag."

*Crandall* (Old English) "from the cranes' valley." Crandell.

*Crawford* (Old English) "from the ford of the crow." Ford.

*Creighton* (Old English) "from the town near the creek." Chricton.

*Crosby* (Scandinavian) "from the shrine of the cross." Coss, Crosbie.

*Cullen* (Celtic) "handsome."  Cullan, Cullie, Cullin.
*Culver* (Old English) "dove."  Cull, Cully.
*Curran* (Celtic) "hero."  Curry.
*Curtis* (Old French) "curteous."  Curt.
*Cutler* (Old English) "knife maker."  Cutty.
*Cyril* (Greek) "lordly."  Cy.
*Cyrus* (Persian) "sun."  Russ.

*Dale* (Teutonic) "from the valley." Dal.

*Dallas* (Celtic) "dweller by the waterfall." Dal.

*Dalton* (Old English) "from the farm in the valley." Tony.

*Damon* (Greek) "constant; tamer." Damian, Damiano, Damien.

*Dana* (Scandinavian) "from Denmark." Dane.

*Daniel* (Hebrew) "God is my judge." Dan, Danny.

*Dante* (Latin) "enduring one."

*Darby* (Celtic) "free man." Dar, Derby.

*Darcy* (Celtic) "dark." D'Arcy, Dar, Darce.

*Darius* (Greek) "wealthy." Derry.

*Darnell* (Old English) "from the hidden place." Dar, Darnall.

*Darrel* (French) "beloved." Dare, Darrell, Darrill, Darryl.

*Darren* (Celtic) "great." Familiar form of Dorian.

*David* (Hebrew) "beloved one." Dave, Davey, Davin.

*Davis* (Scottish) "son of David."

*Dean* (Old English) "from the valley." Deane, Dino.

*Delbert* (Teutonic) "bright as day."  Del, Bert.

*Delmore* (Old French) "from the sea."  Del, Delmar, Delmer.

*Delwin* (Teutonic) "proud friend."  Del, Delwyn.

*Dempster* (Old English) "judge."

*Denby* (Scandinavian) "from the Danish village."  Dennie, Denny.

*Denley* (Old English) "from the valley meadow."

*Dennis* (Greek) "of Dionysus (god of wine and vegetation)."  Dennet, Dennie, Denny, Dion.

*Dennison* (Old English) "son of Dennis."

*Denton* (Old English) "from the valley farm."  Dent.

*Derek* (Teutonic) "ruler of the people."  Darrick, Derrick, Dirk.

*Dermot* (Celtic) "free from envy."  Dermott.

*Derry* (Celtic) "red-haired."

*Desmond* (Celtic) "man from south Munster."  Des.

*Devin* (Celtic) "poet."  Dev.

*Devlin* (Celtic) "brave."

*Dewey* (Welsh) "prized."

*Dewitt* (Old Flemmish) "blond."  DeWitt, Dwight.

*Dexter* (Latin) "dexterous."  Dex.

*Dillon* (Celtic) "faithful."  See also Dylan.

*Dinsmore* (Celtic) "from the hill fort."  Dinnie, Dinny."

*Dominic* (Latin) "belonging to the Lord."  Dom, Domingo, Nick, Nicky.

*Donahue* (Celtic) "dark warrior."  Don, Donohue.

*Donald* (Celtic) "dark stranger." Don, Donn, Donny.
*Donovan* (Celtic) "dark warrior."
*Dorian* (Greek) "from the sea." Darren, Dore, Dorey.
*Douglas* (Celtic) "from the dark water." Doug, Douglass.
*Doyle* (Celtic) "dark stranger."
*Drew* (Old French) "sturdy"; (Old Welsh) "wise." Dru.
*Duane* (Celtic) "little and dark." Dewain, Dwayne.
*Dudley* (Old English) "from the people's meadow."
*Duke* (Latin) "leader; duke."
*Duncan* (Celtic) "dark-skinned warrior." Dunn.
*Dunstan* (Old English) "from the brown stone hill or fortress."
*Durant* (Latin) "enduring." Durand.
*Durward* (Old English) "gate keeper." Derward, Dur, Ward.
*Dustin* (Teutonic) "valiant."
*Dylan* (Welsh) "from the sea."

*Eamon* Irish form of Edmund

*Earl* (Anglo-Saxon) "nobleman." Earle, Errol, Rollo.

*Eaton* (Old English) "from the riverside village."

*Ebenezer* (Hebrew) "rock of help." Eb, Eben.

*Edna* (Celtic) "fiery."

*Edgar* (Anglo-Saxon) "successful spearman." Ed, Eddie, Ned, Ted.

*Edmund* (Anglo-Saxon) "prosperous protector." Edmond.

*Edsel* (Anglo-Saxon) "from the wealthy man's house."

*Edson* (Anglo-Saxon) "son of Edward." Edison.

*Edward* (Anglo-Saxon) "happy protector." Eduardo.

*Edwin* (Anglo-Saxon) "valuable friend." Edlin.

*Egan* (Celtic) "ardent." Egon.

*Egbert* (Teutonic) "bright as a sword." Bert.

*Eleazar* (Hebrew) "God has helped." Eli.

*Eli* (Hebrew) "the highest."

*Elijah* (Hebrew) "Jehovah is God." Eli, Eliot, Elliott, Ellis.

*Elisha* (Hebrew) "the lord is salvation."

*Ellery* (Teutonic) "dweller by the older tree."  Ellary, Ellerey.

*Elliot* (Hebrew) "believes in God."  Eliot.

*Ellison* (Old English) "son of Ellis."

*Ellsworth* (Teutonic) "nobleman's estate."

*Elmer* (Teutonic) "noble; famous."

*Elroy* (Latin) "royal."

*Elston* (Teutonic) "nobleman's town."

*Elton* (Teutonic) "from the old town."  Alden, Eldon.

*Elwin* (Teutonic) "friend of the elves."  Elvis, Elvyn, Elwyn, Win, Winnie.

*Elwood* (Teutonic) "from the old wood."  Ellwood, Woody.

*Elvis* (Scandinavian) "all-wise one."  Alvis.

*Emerson* (Teutonic) "son of the industrious ruler."

*Emery* (Teutonic) "industrious ruler."  Amerigo, Amery, Amory, Emmerich, Emory.

*Emil* (Latin) "flattering; winning."  Emile, Emlen.

*Emmanuel* (Hebrew) "God is with us."  Emanuele, Manuel.

*Emmett* (Anglo-Saxon) "diligent."

*Engelbert* (Teutonic) "bright as an angel."  Bert, Inglebert.

*Enoch* (Hebrew) "dedicated."

*Enos* (Hebrew) "mortal."

*Ephraim* (Hebrew) "doubly fruitful."  Efrem, Ephrem.

*Erasmus* (Greek) "amiable."

*Erastus* (Greek) "beloved."

*Erhard* (Teutonic) "strong resolution."  Erhart.

*Eric* (Scandinavian) "ever-powerful."  Erich, Erik, Rick, Ricky.

*Ernest* (Teutonic) "intent."  Ernesto, Ernie, Ernst.

*Erskine* (Scottish) "from the town of Erskine."  Kin, Kinny.

*Ethan* (Hebrew) "firm."

*Etienne* French form of Stephen.

*Eugene* (Greek) "well-born."  Gene.

*Eustace* (Greek) "fruitful."  Eustis, Stacy.

*Evan* (Celtic) "young warrior."  Welsh form of John.  Ev, Ewen, Owen.

*Evelyn* (French-Teutonic) From "Avelin," meaning ancestor in German.

*Everett* (Teutonic) "strong as the wild boar."  Eberhard, Everard, Eward, Ewart.

*Ezekiel* (Hebrew) "strength of God."  Zeke.

*Ezra* (Hebrew) "helper."

*Fabian* (Latin) "bean farmer."

*Fagen* (Irish Gaelic) "small, fiery one." Fagin.

*Fairfax* (Anglo-Saxon) "fair-haired." Fair, Fax.

*Farley* (Old English) from the bull pasture." Far, Farleigh, Farlie.

*Farrell* (Celtic) "man of valor." Farr, Ferrell.

*Felix* (Latin) "fortunate." Felice.

*Felton* (Old English) "from the farm on the meadow." Felt, Felty.

*Fenton* (Old English) "from the marshland farm." Fen, Fenny.

*Ferdinand* (Teutonic) "adventurous." Ferd, Fergus, Fernando, Hernando.

*Fergus* (Celtic) "strong man."

*Ferris* (Celtic) "Peter, the rock." Irish form of Peter (from Pierce). Farris.

*Fidel* (Latin) "faithful."

*Fielding* (Old English) "from the field." Field.

*Filbert* (Old English) "brilliant." Bert, Phil.

*Filmore* (Old English) "famous."

*Finlay* (Celtic) "little fair-haired soldier." Findlay, Finn.

*Fitzgerald* (Teutonic) "son of the spear-mighty." Fitz, Gerald, Gerry, Jerry.

*Fitzhugh* (Teutonic) "son of the intelligent man." Fitz, Hugh.

*Fitzpatrick* (Teutonic-Latin) "son of a nobleman." Fitz, Patrick.

*Fletcher* (Teutonic) "arrow-featherer, fletcher." Fletch.

*Flint* (Teutonic) "stream."

*Floyd* (Celtic) "the grey."

*Flynn* (Celtic) "son of the red-haired man." Flinn.

*Forbes* (Celtic) "prosperous."

*Ford* (Old English) "river crossing."

*Forrest* (Old French) "forest; woodsman." Forester, Foster.

*Francis* (Teutonic) "free." Chico, Fran, Francesco, Franchot, Francisco, Francois, Frank, Frannie, Frans, Franz, Pancho.

*Franklin* (Teutonic) "free landowner." See also Francis. Franklyn.

*Frazer* (Teutonic) "curly-haired." Fraze, Frazier.

*Frederick* (Teutonic) "peaceful ruler." Eric, Erich, Erik, Fred, Frederic, Frederico, Frederik, Fredric, Fredrick, Friedrich, Fritz, Rick, Ricky.

*Freeman* (Anglo-Saxon) "free man." Free, Freedham.

*Fremont* (Teutonic) "guardian of freedom." Monty.

*Gabriel* (Hebrew) "devoted to God." Gabby, Gabe, Gabrile.

*Gage* (Old French) "pledge."

*Gale* (Celtic) "stranger"; (Old English) "gay; lively." Gael, Gail, Gayle.

*Galen* (Celtic) "intelligent." Gaelan.

*Galvin* (Celtic) "sparrow." Gal, Galvan, Galven.

*Gannon* (Celtic) "fair-complected."

*Gardner* (Teutonic) "gardener." Gar, Gard, Gardiner.

*Garfield* (Teutonic) "battlefield." Gar, Field.

*Garland* (Teutonic) "wreath." Gar, Garlen.

*Garner* (Teutonic) "armed sentry." Gar.

*Garnett* (Teutonic) "armed with a spear"; (Latin) "pomegranate seed; garnet stone." Gar, Garnet.

*Garth* (Norse) "groundskeeper."

*Garvey* (Celtic) "rough peace." Garv.

*Garvin* (Teutonic) "comrade in battle." Gar, Garwin, Vin, Vinny, Win, Winny.

*Garwood* (Teutonic) "from the fir tree forest."  Gar, Wood, Woody.

*Gary* (Teutonic) "spear-carrier."  Garry, Garen."

*Gaston* (French) "man from Gascony."

*Gavin* (Welsh) "white hawk."  Gaven, Gawain."

*Gaylord* (Old French) "gay lord."  Gay, Gaylor."

*Gaynor* (Celtic) "son of the fair-complected man."  Gainer, Gayner.

*Geoffrey* English form of Godfrey; Jeffrey.  Geoff, Jeff.

*George* (Greek) "farmer."  Georg, Giorgio, Jorge.

*Gerald* (Teutonic) "mighty with a spear."  Gary, Gerrie, Gerry, Jerald, Jerrold, Jerry.

*Gerard* (Teutonic) "brave with a spear."  Gerardo, Gerhardt, Gerrie, Gerry.

*Gershom* (Hebrew) "exile."  Gersham.

*Gideon* (Hebrew) "feller of trees; destroyer."

*Gifford* (Teutonic) "bold giver."

*Gilbert* (Teutonic) "trusted."  Bert, Burt, Gib, Gibb, Gil, Wilbert, Wilbur, Wilburt, Will.

*Gilchrist* (Celtic) "servant of Christ."  Gil, Gill.

*Giles* (Greek) "shield-bearer."  Gilles.

*Gilmore* (Celtic) "servant of the Virgin Mary."

*Gilroy* (Celtic) "servant of the red-haired king."  Gil, Roy.

*Gladwin* (Old English) "cheerful friend."  Glad, Win, Winnie.

*Glen* (Gaelic) "valley."  Glenn, Glyn, Glynn.

*Glendon* (Gaelic) "from the dark valley."  Glen, Glenn.

*Goddard* (Teutonic) "divinely firm."  Godard, Godart, Gaddart.

*Godfrey* (Teutonic) "God's peace."  Geoffrey, Geoff.

*Godwon* (Teutonic) "divine friend."  Goodwin, Win, Winnie.

*Gordon* (Old English) "from the triangular hill."  Gordie, Gordy.

*Grady* (Gaelic) "noble; illustrious."

*Granger* (Old English) "farmer."  Grange, Gray.

*Graham* (Old English) "from the gravel-colored estate."

*Grantland* (Old English) "from the large meadow."  Grant.

*Granville* (Old French) "from the large town."  Gran, Grannie.

*Grayson* (Old English) "son of a bailiff."  Gray, Son, Sonny.

*Gregory* (Greek) "Watchman."  Greg, Gregg, Gregor, Gregorio.

*Grey* (Old English) "of the grey-haired man."

*Griffin* (Latin) "griffin (a mythical beast)."  Griff.

*Griffith* (Old Welsh) "fierce chief."

*Griswold* (Teutonic) "from the gray forest."

*Grover* (Old English) "from the grove."

*Gunther* (Old Norse) "warrior."  Gun, Gunnar, Gunner, Gunter.

*Gustave* (Swedish) "staff of the Goths."  Gus, Gustaf, Gustav.

*Guthrie* (Celtic) "war serpent."

*Guy* (French) "guide"; (Teutonic) "warrior"; (Celtic) "sensible."

*Hadley* (Old English) "from the heath."  Had, Lee, Leigh.

*Haldan* (Teutonic) "half-Danish."  Dan, Danny, Don, Donny, Hal.

*Hale* (Teutonic) "robust."  Hal.

*Haley* (Gaelic) "ingenious."  Hal, Hale, Lee, Leigh.

*Hall* (Old English) "from the hall."

*Halsey* (Old English) "from Hal's island."  Hal.

*Halstead* (Old English) "from the manor."  Hal, Halstead.

*Hamilton* (Norman) "from the beautiful mountain."  Ham, Hamil, Tony.

*Hamlin* (Teutonic) "ruler of the home."  Ham, Lin, Lynn.

*Hans* Scandinavian form of John.

*Harcourt* (Old French) "fortified dwelling."  Harry, Court.

*Hardan* (Old English) "from the land of hares."  Harding.

*Harding* (Old English) "hardy and brave."

*Hardy* (Teutonic) "bold and daring."

*Harlan* (Teutonic) "from the land of warriors."  Harland, Harlin.

*Harley* (Old English) "from the meadow." Arley.

*Harlow* (Old English) "from the rough hill." Alro.

*Harmon* English form of Herman.

*Harold* (Teutonic) "army-ruler." Hal, Harry.

*Harper* (Old English) "harp player." Harp.

*Harrison* (Old English) "son of Harry." Harris.

*Hartley* (Old English) "from the deer meadow." Hart.

*Harvey* (Teutonic) "warrior." Harv, Herve, Hervey.

*Haslett* (Teutonic) "from the hazel tree land." Haze, Hazlett.

*Hastings* (Teutonic) "son of a stern man." Hastie, Hasty.

*Hayden* (Old English) "from the hedged place."

*Haywood* (Old English) "from the hedged forest." Heywood, Woodie, Woody.

*Heath* (Middle English) "from the heath." Heathcliff.

*Hector* (Greek) "steadfast." Etor, Hechtor, Heck.

*Henry* (Teutonic) "ruler of an estate." Enrico, Hal, Hank, Harry, Heinrich, Hendrik, Henri.

*Herbert* (Teutonic) "bright soldier." Bert, Bertie, Harbert, Herbert, Herb, Herbie.

*Herman* (Teutonic) "warrior." Armand, Armin, Harmon, Hermann.

*Hernando* Spanish form of Ferdinand.

*Hershel* (Hebrew) "deer." Herschel, Hersh, Hirsch.

*Hewett* (Teutonic) "little and intelligent." Hewitt.

*Hilary* (Latin) "cheerful."  Hi, Hilaire, Hill, Hillary, Hillie, Hilly.

*Hillard* (Teutonic) "brave warrior."  Hill, Hillyer.

*Hiram* (Hebrew) "exalted."  Hy.

*Hobart* (Teutonic) "bright-minded."  Hobard.

*Holbrook* (Old English) "from the brook in the hollow."  Brook, Holbrooke.

*Holder* (Teutonic) "gracious."  Holden.

*Hollis* (Old English) "from the grove of holly trees."  Hollings.

*Holmes* (Teutonic) "from the river islands."

*Holt* (Old English) "from the forest."

*Homer* (Greek) "promise."

*Horace* (Latin) "keeper of the hours."  Horatio.

*Hosea* (Hebrew) "salvation."

*Howard* (Teutonic) "watchman."  Howie, Ward.

*Howland* (Old English) "from the hills."  Howell.

*Hoyt* (Old English) "small boat."  Hoyle, Hoit.

*Hubert* (Teutonic) "bright-minded."  Bert, Hobart, Huberto, Hubie, Hugh, Hugo.

*Hugh* (Teutonic) "intelligence."  Huey, Hughie, Hugo.

*Hume* (Scandinavian) "from the grass hill."

*Humbert* (Teutonic) "brilliant Hun."  Hum.

*Humphrey* (Teutonic) "peaceful Hun."  Hum, Humfrey, Onofredo.

*Hunter* (Old English) "hunter."  Hunt.

*Huntington* (Old English) "hunting estate." Hunt, Huntingdon.
*Huntley* (Old English) "hunter's meadow." Hunt, Lee, Leigh.
*Hurley* (Celtic) "sea-tide."
*Huxley* (Old English) "from the Hugh's meadow." Hux, Lee, Leigh.
*Hyatt* (Old English) "from the high gate."
*Hyman* English form of Chaim. Hy, Manny.

*Iago* (Spanish; Welsh) Form of James.

*Ian* Scottish form of John.

*Ichabod* (Scottish Gaelic) "where is his glory?"

*Ignatius* (Latin) "fiery; ardent." Iggy, Ignance, Ignacio.

*Ingemar* (Old Norse) "famous son." Ingamar, Ingmar.

*Inger* (Old Norse) "son's army." Igor, Ingar.

*Innis* (Celtic) "from the island." Inness.

*Ira* (Hebrew) "descendant."

*Irving* (Celtic) "beautiful"; (Old English) "sea friend." Erv, Ervin, Erwin, Irv, Irwin.

*Isaac* (Hebrew) "he who laughs." Ike, Isaak.

*Isadore* (Greek) "gift of Isis." Dore, Dory.

*Isiah* (Hebrew) "salvation of God." Isa.

*Ishmael* (Hebrew) "God hears."

*Israel* (Hebrew) "soldier for the Lord."

*Itamar* (Hebrew) "one from the island of palms."

*Ivan* Russian form of John.
*Ivar* (Scandinavian) "archer."  Igor, Iver, Ivor.

*Jackson* (Old English) "son of Jack." Jack.

*Jacob* (Hebrew) "supplanter." Cobb, Jack, Jacques, Jaime, Jake, Jamie, Jay, Jayme, Jim, Jimmie, Jimmy, Seamus, Shamus.

*Jacques* French form of Jacob. James.

*Jaime* Spanish form of James.

*James* English form of Jacob (from Jaime). Jacques, Jaime, Jamie, Jay, Jayme, Jim, Jimmy, Seamus, Shamus.

*Jan* Dutch and Slavic form of John. Janos.

*Jared* Hebrew form of Jordan. Jerad.

*Jarek* (Slavic) "one born in January."

*Jarvis* (Teutonic) "keen as a spear." Jervis.

*Jason* (Greek) "healer." Jay, Jayson.

*Jasper* English form of Casper (from Gaspar).

*Jean* French form of John.

*Jed* (Hebrew) "beloved of the Lord." A short form of Jedidiah. Jedd.

*Jefferson* (Old English) "son of Jeffrey." Jeff, Jeffie.

*Jeffrey* (Old French) "heavenly peace."  Geoff, Geoffrey, Godfrey, Gottfried, Jeff, Jeffery.

*Jeremiah* (Hebrew) "appointed by Jehovah."  Jere, Jereme, Jeremy, Jerry.

*Jerome* (Latin) "holy name."  Gerrie, Gerry, Jere, Jereme, Jerry.

*Jesse* (Hebrew) "gift of God."  Jess, Jessie.

*Jethro* (Hebrew) "preeminence."  Jeth.

*Joachim* (Hebrew) "the Lord will judge."  Joaquin.

*Joel* (Hebrew) "Jehovah is God."

*John* (Hebrew) "God's precious gift."  Evan, Ewen, Hans, Ian, Jack, Jackie, Jan, Janos, Jean, Jens, Jock, Jocko, Johann, Johannes, Johnnie, Johnny, Jon, Juan, Owen, Sean, Shuan, Shawn, Zane.

*Jonah* (Hebrew) "dove."  Jonas.

*Jonathan* (Hebrew) "Jehovah gave."  Jon, Jonathon.

*Jordan* (Hebrew) "descender."  Jared, Jerad, Jourdain.

*Joseph* (Hebrew) "he shall add."  Che, Guiseppe, Jo, Joe, Joey, Jose.

*Joshua* (Hebrew) "Jehovah saves."  Josh.

*Josiah* (Hebrew) "Jehovah supports."

*Joyce* (Teutonic) "of the Goths."  Jocelyn.

*Judah* (Hebrew) "praised."  Jud, Judd, Jude.

*Jules* French form of Julius.  Jule.

*Julian* (Latin) "belonging or related to Julius."

*Julius* (Greek) "youthful and downy-bearded."  Jule, Jules, Julie.

*Justin* (Latin) "upright."  Justinian, Justis, Justus.

*Kane* (Celtic) "fair; bright." Kain, Kaine, Kayne.

*Karl* German form of Charles.

*Keane* (Old English) "sharp; keen." See also Keenan, Kean, Keene.

*Kearney* Form of Carney.

*Keefe* (Celtic) "cherished; handsome."

*Keegan* (Celtic) "fiery."

*Keenan* (Celtic) "little and innocent." Keane, Keen, Kienan.

*Kein* (Celtic) "dark-skinned."

*Keith* (Welsh) "wood-dweller."

*Kelly* (Celtic) "warrior." Kelley.

*Kelsey* (Teutonic) "dweller by the water."

*Kendall* (Celtic) "from the bright valley." Ken, Kendal, Kendell, Kenny.

*Kendrick* (Anglo-Saxon) "son of Henry"; (Old English) "royal ruler." Ken, Rick.

*Kennedy* (Celtic) "helmeted chief."

*Kenneth* (Celtic) "handsome"; (Old English) "royal oath." Ken, Kenny.

*Kent* (Welsh) "white; bright."  Short form of Kenton.

*Kenton* (Old English) "from the farm in Kent."  Ken, Kenn, Kent.

*Kenyon* (Gaelic) "white-haired; blond."

*Kermit* (Celtic) "free man."  Ker, Kerr.

*Kerry* (Celtic) "dark."

*Kevin* (Celtic) "gentle; kind."

*Kieran* (Irish Gaelic) "dark, black one."

*Killian* (Celtic) "little and warlike."  Killian, Killy.

*Kim* (Welsh) "chief."

*Kimball* (Anglo-Saxon) "warrior chief; royal and bold."

*Kinglsey* (Old English) "from the king's meadow."  King, Kinsley.

*Kingston* (Old English) "from the king's manor."

*Kipp* (Old English) "from the pointed hill."  Kip, Kipper.

*Kirby* (Teutonic) "from the church village."

*Kirk* (Scandinavian) "from the church."  Kirke.

*Kit* Familiar form of Christopher.

*Knight* (Middle English) "a knight or soldier."

*Knute* Danish form of Canute.

*Kohler* (German) "one who burns charcoal."

*Kurt* German form of Conrad.

*Kyle* (Celtic) "handsome; from the strait."  Ky.

*Laban* (Hebrew) "white one."

*Ladd* (Middle English) "attendant." Lad, Laddie.

*Laird* (Scottish) "landed proprietor; laird."

*Lamar* (Teutonic) "famous throughout the land."

*Lambert* (Teutonic) "bright as the land." Bert, Lamberto.

*Lamont* (Scandinavian) "lawyer." Lammond, Monty.

*Lance* (Teutonic) "land." Lancelot, Lanzo.

*Lane* (Old English) "from the narrow road." Lanie, Layne.

*Lang* (Scandinavian) "tall one."

*Langdon* (Old English) "from the long hill." Landon, Langston.

*Lars* Scandinavian form of Lawrence. Larsen, Larson.

*Latham* (Teutonic) "dweller and the barn."

*Lathrop* (Old English) "from the village of barns."

*Latimer* (Anglo-French) "interpreter." Lat, Latty.

*Lawford* (Old English) "from the ford on the hill." Law, Ford.

*Lawrence* (Latin) "laurel-crowned." Larry, Lars, Lauren, Laurence, Laurens, Laurent, Laurie, Lon, Lonny, Loren,Lorenzo, Lorin, Lorrie, Lorry, Rance.

*Lawton* (Old English) "from the estate on the hill."

*Lazarus* (Hebrew) "God will help." Lazar.

*Leander* (Greek) "lionlike." Ander, Lee, Leigh, Leo.

*Leif* (Old Norse) "beloved." Lief.

*Leighton* (Old English) "from the meadow farm."

*Leland* (Old English) "from the meadow land." Lee, Leigh.

*Lemuel* (Hebrew) "dedicated to the Lord." Lem.

*Leo* (Latin) "lion." Short form of Leander; Leonard; Leopold. Lee, Leon, Lev.

*Leon* (French) "lion; lionlike." French form of Leo. Short form of Leonard; Napolean. Leon.

*Leonard* (Teutonic) "bold lion." See also Leander. Lee, Len, Lenny, Leo, Leon, Lonny.

*Leopold* (Teutonic) "Patriotic."

*Leroy* (French-Latin) "royal." Elroy, Lee, Leigh, Roy.

*Leslie* (Celtic) "from the gray fort." Lee, Leigh, Les.

*Lester* (Latin) "from the camp of the legion"; (Old English) "from Leicester."

*Levi* (Hebrew) "united."

*Lewis* Short form of Llewellyn. Form of Louis. Lew.

*Liam* Irish form of William.

*Lincoln* (Celtic-Latin) "from the settlement by the pool." Linc, Link.

*Lindsay* (Old English) "from the island of serpents." Lind, Lindsey.

*Linus* (Greek) "flaxen-haired."

*Lionel* (Latin) "lionlike."

*Llewellyn* (Celtic) "lionlike; ruler." Lew, Lewis.

*Lloyd* (Celtic) "gray." Floyd, Loy.

*Locke* (Old English) "from the forest." Lock.

*Logan* (Celtic) "from the hollow."

*Lombard* (Teutonic) "long-bearded." Bard, Barr.

*Lorimer* (Latin) "harness-maker." Lorrie, Lorrimer, Lorry.

*Loring* (Old High German) "son of the famous warrior." Lorrie, Lorry.

*Louis* (Teutonic) "renowned warrior." Aloysius, Lew, Lewis, Lou, Louie, Ludwig, Luigi, Luis.

*Lowell* (Old English) "beloved." Lovell, Lowe.

*Lucius* (Latin) "bringer of light." Lucas, Lucias, Lucian, Lukas, Luke.

*Luther* (Teutonic) "famous warrior."

*Lyle* (French-Latin) "from the island." Lisle.

*Lyman* (Old English) "a man from the valley."

*Lyndon* (Teutonic) "from the linden tree hill." Lin, Lindon, Lindy, Lyn, Lynn.

*Lynn* (Old English) "dweller by the waterfall." Lin, Linn, Lyn.

*Mac* (Celtic) "son of." Short form of names beginning with "mac"; "max"; "mc." Mack, Macauly, Macawley.

*Mackenzie* (Celtic) "son of the wise leader." Mac, Mack.

*Macklin* (Celtic) "son of Flann, the red-haired."

*Macnair* (Celtic) "son of the heir."

*Maddox* (Celtic) "beneficient."

*Madison* (Teutonic) "son of the mighty soldier." Maddie, Sonny.

*Magnus* (Latin) "great." Manus.

*Maitland* (Old English) "dweller in the meadow."

*Major* (Latin) "greater." Mayer, Mayor."

*Malachi* (Hebrew) "angel." Mal, Malachy.

*Malcolm* (Celtic) "follower of St. Columba (an early Scottish saint)." Mal.

*Mallory* (Teutonic) "army counselor." Mal.

*Manfred* (Teutonic) "man of peace." Fred, Freddie, Mannie, Manny.

*Marcel* (Latin) "little and warlike." Marcellus.

*Mark* (Latin) "hammer."  Marc, Marcos, Marcus, Mario, Marius.

*Marlow* (Old English) "from the hill by the lake."  Marlowe.

*Marshall* (Old French) "steward; horse-keeper."  Marsh, Marshal.

*Martin* (Latin) "warlike."  Martie, Martino, Marty.

*Marvin* (Teutonic) "lover of the sea."  Marve, Marwin, Mervin, Merwin, Meryn.

*Mason* (French-Teutonic) "stone-worker."  Mace, Sonny.

*Matthew* (Hebrew) "gift of God."  Mathias, Matt, Matthias, Mattie, Matty.

*Maurice* (Latin) "dark-skinned."  Maurie, Maury, Morey, Morris.

*Max* Short form of Maximilian.

*Maximilian* (Latin) "the greatest."  Mac, Mack, Max, Maxie.

*Maxwell* (Anglo-Saxon) "from the rich man's well."

*Maynard* (Teutonic) "powerful; brave."  May, Mayne, Menard.

*Mead* (Old English) "from the meadow."  Meade.

*Melbourne* (Old English) "from the mill stream."  Mel, Melburn.

*Melville* (Old English-French) "from the estate of the hard worker."  Mel.

*Melvin* (Celtic) "chief."  Mel, Melvyn, Vinnie.

*Mendel* (Greek) "knowledge; wisdom."  Mendy.

*Meredith* (Old Welsh) "protection from the sea."  Merideth, Merry.

*Merlin* (French-Latin) "falcon."  Marlin, Marlon, Merle.

*Merrill* (Teutonic) "famous."  Merill, Meryl.

*Meyer* (Teutonic) "farmer." Meier, Meir, Myer.

*Michael* (Hebrew) "like unto the Lord." Micah, Michal, Michail, Michele, Mickey, Miguel, Mike, Mischa, Mitch, Mitchel, Mitchell.

*Miles* (Latin) "soldier." Milo, Myles.

*Millard* (Latin) "keeper of the mill."

*Milton* (Old English) "from the mill town." Milt.

*Monroe* (Celtic) "from the mouth of the Roe River." Munroe.

*Montague* (French) "from the pointed mountain." Monte, Monty.

*Montgomery* (Old English) "from the rich man's mountain." Monte, Monty.

*Mordecai* (Hebrew) "belonging to Marduk." Mord, Mordy, Mort, Mortie.

*Morris* (Latin) "dark-skinned."

*Mortimer* (French-Latin) "dweller by the still water." Mort.

*Moses* (Hebrew) "saved from the water." Moise, Mose, Moshe, Moss.

*Muhammad* (Arabic) "praised." A Muslim saying: "If you have a hundred sons, name them all Muhammad." There are more than 500 variations of this name; it is the most common boy's name in the world.

*Murdock* (Celtic) "wealthy seaman."

*Murray* (Celtic) "sailor."

*Myron* (Greek) "fragrant ointment." Ron, Ronnie.

*Napoleon* (Italian) "from Naples." Leon, Nap, Nappie, Nappy.
*Nathaniel* (Hebrew) "gift of God." Nat, Nate, Nathan, Nathanael.
*Nehemiah* (Hebrew) "confronted by the Lord."
*Neil* (Celtic) "champion." Neal, Neale, Neill, Neils, Niel, Niels, Niles.
*Nelson* (English) "son of Neil." Nealson, Neils, Nels, Nelson, Nils, Nilson.
*Nestor* (Greek) "wisdom."
*Neville* (Latin) "from the new town." Nev, Nevil.
*Nevin* (Celtic) "worshipper of the saint"; (Teutonic) "nephew." Nevins, Niven.
*Newlin* (Celtic) "from the new spring."
*Newton* (Anglo-Saxon) "from the new farmstead."
*Nicholas* (Greek) "the people's victory." Claus, Cole, Colin, Niccolo, Nick, Nicky, Nicol, Nicolai, Nicolas, Nikita, Nikki, Nixon.
*Niels* (Scandinavian) Nels, Nils, Nielsen, Nilsson.
*Nigel* (Latin) "dark."

*Noah* (Hebrew) "rest."

*Noel* (French-Latin) "born at Christmas."

*Nolan* (Celtic) "famous; noble." Noland.

*Norbert* (Tuetonic) "brilliant hero." Bert, Bertie, Norb.

*Norman* (Teutonic) "man from the north." Norm.

*Norris* (French-Latin) "caretaker."

*Northrop* (Anglo-Saxon) "from the north farm."

*Norton* (Anglo-Saxon) "from the northern village."

*Norwood* (Teutonic) "guirdian of the north gate."

*Nye* (Old English) "from the island."

*Oakes* (Old English) "from the oak trees." Oak, Oakley.

*Obadiah* (Hebrew) "servant of God." Obie.

*Odell* (Norse) "man of property." Dell, Ody.

*Ogden* (Old English) "from the oak tree valley."

*Olaf* (Old Norse) "ancestral talisman relic." Olav, Ole, Olen, Olin.

*Oleg* (Russian) "holy one."

*Oliver* (Latin) "olive tree symbolizing peace." Noll, Olivero, Olivier, Ollie.

*Omar* (Arabic) "first son; follower of the prophet."

*Ordway* (Anglo-Saxon) "warrior with spear."

*Oren* (Celtic) "pale." Oran, Orin, Orren, Orrin.

*Orestes* (Greek) "mountain man."

*Orion* (Celtic) "son of fire."

*Orland* (Teutonic) "from the famed land." Lnad, Lanny, Orlan, Orlando.

*Ormond* (Teutonic) "mariner."

*Orrick* (Old English) "from near the old oak." Rick.

*Orson* (Latin) "bearlike; strong." Sonny.
*Orton* (Teutonic) "wealthy."
*Orville* (Old French) "from the golden estate." Orval, Ory.
*Osborn* (Teutonic) "divine bear." Osbourne, Ozzie.
*Oscar* (Celtic) "leaping spearman." Askar, Ozzie.
*Osgood* (Teutonic) "divine creator."
*Osmond* (Teutonic) "divine protector." Osmund.
*Oswald* (Teutonic) "having power from God." Oswell, Ozzie, Waldo.
*Otis* (Greek) "keen of hearing." Oates.
*Otto* (Teutonic) "prosperous." Othello.
*Owen* (Celtic) "young warrior."
*Oxford* (Old English) "from the river crossing of the oxen." Ford.

*Pablo* Spanish form of Paul.

*Paco* Spanish form of Francisco.  Pancho.

*Page* (French) "youthful attendent."  Padgett, Paige.

*Paine* (Latin) "from the country."  Payne.

*Palmer* (Old English) "palm-bearing pilgrim."

*Parker* (Middle English) "guardian of the park."  Park, Parke.

*Parnell* (French) "little Peter."  Nell.

*Parrish* (Middle English) "from the churchyard."  Parry.

*Pascal* (Italian) "born at Easter of Passover."  Pascale, Pasquale.

*Patrick* (Latin) "nobleman."  Paddy, Padriac, Pat, Paton, Patrice, Patsy, Patty.

*Patton* (Old English) "from the warrior's estate."

*Paul* (Latin) "small."  Pablo, Paulie.

*Pembroke* (Welsh) "from the headland."

*Penn* (Teutonic) "commander."  Short form of Penrod.  Pennie, Penny.

*Penrod* (Teutonic) "famous commander."  Pen, Penn, Rod, Roddy.

*Percival* (Old French) "pierce-the-valley"; (Greek) "destroyer."  Percy.

*Perry* (Old English) "pear tree"; (Old French) "little Peter."

*Peter* (Greek) "rock."  Farris, Ferris, Patty, Pedro, Peirce, Perkin, Perry, Pete, Pierce, Pierre, Pietro.

*Peyton* (Old English) "from the warrior's estate."  Payron.

*Phelps* (Old English) "son of Philip."

*Philip* (Greek) "lover of horses."  Felipe, Phil, Phillip, Phillipe.

*Phinens* (Hebrew) "oracle."

*Pierrepont* (French-Latin) "dweller by the stone bridge."  Pierre.

*Plato* (Greek) "strong-shouldered."

*Pomeroy* (Old French) "from the apple orchard."  Pom, Roy.

*Porter* (Latin) "keeper of the gate."

*Prentice* (Latin) "apprentice; learner."  Pren.

*Prescott* (Old English) "from the priest's cottage."  Scott, Scotty.

*Presley* (Old English) "from the priest's meadow."  Priestly.

*Preston* (Old English) "from the priest's estate."

*Price* (Welsh) "son of the ardent one."  Brice, Bryce, Pryce.

*Primo* (Italian) "firstborn."

*Prince* (Latin) "princelike."

*Pryor* (Latin) "head of a monastery; prior."  Pry

*Putnam* (Old English) "from near the pond."  Putnem.

*Quartus* (Latin) "the fourth child."
*Quentin* (Latin) "fifth child."  Quent, Quinn, Quint.
*Quillan* (Celtic) "cub."  Quill.
*Quinby* (Scandinavian) "from the woman's estate."  Quim, Quin.
*Quincy* (Old French) "from the fifth son's estate."  Quinn, Quinzey.
*Quinlan* (Celtic) "physically strong."
*Quinton* (Old English) "from the estate of the queen."

*Radburn* (Old English) "from the red stream." Rad, Radborne, Radbourne.

*Radcliffe* (Old English) "from the red cliff." Rad, Cliff.

*Rafael* Spanish form of Raphael. Rafe, Rafi, Raffin.

*Rafferty* (Celtic) "prosperous." Rafe.

*Raleigh* (Old English) "from the deer meadow." Lee, Leigh, Rawley.

*Ralph* (Old English) "protector." Rolph.

*Ramon* Spanish form of Raymond.

*Ramsay* (Teutonic) "from the ram's island; from the raven's island." Ram, Ramsey.

*Randall* Modern form of Randolph. Rand, Randell, Randy.

*Randolph* (Teutonic) "shield-wolf." Rand, Randall, Randell, Randolph, Randy.

*Ransom* (Old English) "son of the shield."

*Raphael* (Hebrew) "divine healer." Rafael, Rafe, Ray.

*Rayburn* (Old English) "from the deer brook." Burn, Burny, Ray.

*Raymond* (Teutonic) "mighty or wise protector." Raimundo, Ramon, Ray, Raymund.

*Raynor* (Old Norse) "mighty army." Ragnor.

*Redford* (Old English) "from the red river crossing." Ford, Red.

*Reece* (Welsh) "enthusiastic." Rees, Rhys, Rice, Rhett.

*Reed* (Old English) "red-haired." Reade, Reid.

*Reeve* (Middle English) "steward."

*Regan* (Celtic) "kingly." Reagan, Reagen.

*Reginald* (Teutonic) "powerful and mighty." Reg, Reggie, Reinald, Reihold, Renault, Rene, Reynolds, Rinaldo.

*Remington* (Teutonic) "from the raven estate." Tony.

*Rene* (French) "reborn." French short form of Reginald.

*Renfred* (Teutonic) "peacemaker."

*Reuben* (Greek) "behold, a son." Rube, Ruben, Rubin.

*Rex* (Latin) "king."

*Reynard* (Old French) "fox." Ray, Raynard, Reinhard, Renard, Renaud, Rey.

*Richard* (Teutonic) "powerful ruler." Dick , Ric, Ricardo, Rich, Richie, Rick, Ricki, Ricky, Rico, Riki.

*Richmond* (Teutonic) "mighty protector."

*Ridley* (Old English) "from the red meadow."

*Riley* (Celtic) "valiant." Reilly.

*Riordan* (Celtic) "royal poet." Dan, Danny.

*Ripley* (Anglo-Saxon) "from the shouter's meadow."  Lee, Leigh, Rip.

*Roarke* (Celtic) "famous ruler."

*Robert* (Teutonic) "bright fame."  Bob, Bobby, Rab, Rip, Rob, Robb, Robbie, Robby, Roberto, Robin, Rupert.

*Robinson* (English) "son of Robert."  Robin.

*Rocco* (Old German) "one who rests."  Roch, Rock.

*Rochester* (Teutonic) "from the stone camp."  Chester, Chet, Rocky.

*Rockwell* (Old English) "from the rocky spring."

*Roderick* (Teutonic) "famous ruler."  Rod, Roddy, Roderic, Rodrigo, Rodrique, Rory.

*Rodman* (Old English) "dweller by the cross."  Rod, Roddy.

*Rodney* (Teutonic) "famous."

*Rogan* (Irish Gaelic) "red-haired one."  Ronan, Rooney, Rowney.

*Roger* (Teutonic) "famous spearman."  Rodge, Rodger, Rog, Rogers, Rutger.

*Roland* (Teutonic) "from the famous land."  Lanny, Rollie, Rollins, Rollo, Rowland.

*Roman* (Latin) "from Rome."  Romain.

*Romeo* (Italian) "pilgrim to Rome."

*Ronald* Scottish form of Reginald.

*Rooney* (Celtic) "red-haired."  Rowan, Rowen.

*Rory* (Celtic) "red king."

*Roscoe* (Teutonic) "from the deer forest."  Ross, Coe.

*Ross* (Old French) "red"; (Scottish Gaelic) "headland."

*Roy* (Old French) "king."

*Royal* (Old French) "kingly."

*Royce* (Old English) "son of the king."

*Rudolph* (Teutonic) "famous wolf." Raoul, Rolf, Rolfe, Rollo, Rudie, Rudolf, Rudy.

*Rudyard* (Old English) "from the red enclosure." Rudd, Rudy.

*Rufus* (Latin) "red-haired." Rufe.

*Russell* (Latin) "red-haired; fox-colored."

*Rutherford* (Old English) "from the cattle ford."

*Rutledge* (Old English) "from the red pool."

*Ryan* (Irish Gaelic) "little king."

*Sacha* (Russian) "helper of men." Sasha.

*Salvatore* (Italian) "savior." Sal, Salvador.

*Samson* (Hebrew) "resplendent." Sam, Sammy, Sansome.

*Samuel* (Hebrew) "asked of God." Sam, Samuele, Shem.

*Sanborn* (Old English) "from the sandy brook." Sandy.

*Sancho* (Latin) "sanctified."

*Sanders* (Greek) "son of Alexander." Sandor, Saunders.

*Sanford* (Old English) "from the sandy cord." Sandy.

*Sargent* (Old French-Latin) "army officer." Sarge, Sergeant, Sergent."

*Saul* (Hebrew) "longed for." Sol, Solly, Zolly.

*Sawyer* (Celtic) "sawyer of wood."

*Saxon* (Old English) "swordsman." Sax.

*Schuyler* (Dutch) "scholar." Sky.

*Scott* (Old English) "Scotsman." Scot, Scottie.

*Seamus* Irish form of James. Shamus.

*Sean* Irish form of John. Shane, Shaun, Shawn.

*Searle* (Teutonic) "wearing armor."

*Sebastian* (Greek) "revered." Bastien, Sebastien.

*Selby* (Teutonic) "from the manor farm."

*Seldon* (Teutonic) "from the valley." Don, Donny.

*Selwyn* (Anglo-Saxon) "friend from the palace." Selwin, Winnie, Wynn.

*Serge* (Latin) "attendant." Sergio.

*Seth* (Hebrew) "the appointed."

*Seward* (Anglo-Saxon) "guardian of the seacoast."

*Seymour* (Old French) "from St. Maur." Morey, Morrie.

*Shannon* (Celtic) "small and wise."

*Shaw* (Old English) "from the shady grove."

*Sheehan* (Celtic) "little and peaceful."

*Sheffield* (Old English) "from the crooked field." Field, Sheff.

*Shelby* (Anglo-Saxon) "from the ledge farm." Shell, Shelly.

*Sheldon* (Old English) "from the farm on the ledge." Shell, Shelley, Shelton.

*Sheridan* (Celtic) "wild man."

*Sherlock* (Old English) "fair-haired."

*Sherman* (Old English) "shearer." Manny, Sherm.

*Sherwin* (Old English) "swift runner." Win, Winnie.

*Sherwood* (Old English) "from the bright forest." Wood, Woody.

*Sidney* (Old French) "from St. Denys." Sid.

*Sigfried* (Teutonic) "victorious peace."  Sig, Sigfrid.

*Sigmund* (Teutonic) "victorious protector."  Sig.

*Silas* (Latin) "man of the forest."  Silvain, Sylvan.

*Simon* (Hebrew) "he who hears."  Si, Simeon, Simone.

*Sinclair* (Old French) "from St. Clair."  Clair, Claire.

*Sloan* (Celtic) "warrior."  Sloane.

*Solomon* (Hebrew) "peaceful."  Shalom, Sol, Solly.

*Spencer* (Old English; Latin) "dispenser of provisions."  Spence.

*Sprague* (Teutonic) "lively."

*Stacy* (Latin) "stable; dependable."

*Stanfield* (Old English) "from the stony field."

*Stanford* (Old English) "from the landing ford."  Stan, Ford.

*Stanislaus* (Slavic) "glory of the camp."  Stan, Stanislaw.

*Stanley* (Old English) "dweller at stony meadow."  Stan.

*Stanton* (Old English) "from the stone dwelling."

*Stephen* (Greek) "crown."  Etienne, Esteban, Stefan, Stefano, Stephan, Steve, Steven.

*Sterling* (Old English) "of honest value."

*Stillman* (Anglo-Saxon) "quiet man."

*Stuart* (Old English) "caretaker; steward."  Steward, Stewart, Stu.

*Sullivan* (Celtic) "black-eyed."

*Sumner* (French-Latin) "church officer; summoner."

*Sutton* (Old English) "from the south village."

*Sven* (Scandinavia) "youth."  Svein, Svend, Swen.
*Sylvester* (Latin) "from the woods."

*Tab* (Spanish-Arabic) "drummer." Tabb, Tabby.

*Talbot* (Old French) "valley-bright."

*Tanner* (Old English) "leather worker; tanner." Tann, Tanny.

*Tate* (Middle English) "cheerful."

*Tavish* (Celtic) "twin." Tavis, Tevis.

*Taylor* (French-Latin) "tailor."

*Teague* (Celtic) "bard."

*Templeton* (Old English) "from the town of the temple." Temp, Temple.

*Terence* (Latin) "tender"; (Celtic) "like a tall tower." Terrence, Terry.

*Thaddeus* (Greek) "courageous"; (Hebrew) "the praised." Tad, Tadd, Thad.

*Thatcher* (Old English) "roofer; thactcher." Thaxter.

*Thayer* (Teutonic) "from the nation's army."

*Theobald* (Teutonic) "patriotic." Ted, Tedd, Teddy, Thebault, Theo.

*Theodore* (Greek) "divine gift." Ted, Tedd, Teddy.

*Theodoric* (Teutonic) "ruler of the people." Derek, Dirk, Dieter, Dietrich.

*Thomas* (Hebrew) "twin." Tam, Tammy, Thoma, Tom, Tomaso, Tomkin, Tomlin, Tommie, Tommy.

*Thorndike* (Old English) "from the thorny embankment." Thorn.

*Thornton* (Old English) "from the thorn tree farm." Thorn.

*Thorpe* (Teutonic) "from the hamlet."

*Thurston* (Scandinavian) "Thor's stone or jewel."

*Timothy* (Greek) "honoring God." Tim, Timmie, Timmy.

*Titus* (Greek) "giant"; (Latin) "safe." Tito.

*Tobias* (Hebrew) "goodness of the Lord." Tobe, Tobie, Tobin, Toby.

*Todd* (Middle English) "fox."

*Torrance* (Celtic) "from the tower." Torey, Torr, Torrence, Torry.

*Townsend* (Old English) "from the town's end." Town, Townie.

*Tracy* (Celtic) "battler"; (Latin) "courageous." Tracey.

*Trahern* (Celtic) "strong as iron." Tray.

*Travis* (French-Latin) "from the crossroads." Traver, Travers.

*Trent* (Latin) "dweller by the river front."

*Trevor* (Celtic) "prudent." Trev.

*Tristan* (Latin) "sorrowful." Tris, Tristram.

*Troy* (Celtic) "foot soldier."

*Truman* (Old English) "faithful man."

*Tucker* (Old English) "tucker of cloth." Tuck.

*Tyler* (Old English) "maker of tiles."
*Tynan* (Celtic) "dark." Ty.
*Tyrone* (Greek) "sovereign"; (Celtic) "land of Owen." Ty.
*Tyrus* English form of Thor. Ty.
*Tyson* (Teutonic) "son of the Teuton."

*Uan* (Irish Gaelic) "lamblike."

*Udell* (Old English) "from the yew tree valley." Del, Dell.

*Ugo* (Italian) "intelligent one." Hugo.

*Uland* (Teutonic) "from the noble land."

*Ulf* (Sweedish) "wolflike one." Ulfreed, Ulv.

*Ulric* (Teutonic) "wolf-ruler." Ric, Rick, Ricky, Ulrich, Ulrick.

*Ulysses* (Greek) "wrathful." Ulick, Ulises.

*Upton* (Anglo-Saxon) "from the upper town."

*Urban* (Latin) "from the city; courteous."

*Uriah* (Hebrew) "the light is my Jehovah."

*Uriel* (Hebrew) "Jehovah is my light." Uri, Yuri.

*Urs* (Latin) "bearlike." Urson.

*Uzziel* (Hebrew) "one with the power of God." Uzi, Uziel.

*Vachel* (Old French) "one who keeps cows."

*Vail* (French-Latin) "from the valley."

*Valentine* (Latin) "strong; healthy." Val.

*Van* (Dutch) "from." Short from of many Dutch surnames.

*Vance* (Middle English) "thresher."

*Vassily* (Russian) "definitive guardian."

*Vaughn* (Celtic) "small." Vaughan.

*Vernon* (Latin) "flourishing." Lavern, Vern, Verne.

*Victor* (Latin) "conqueror." Vic, Vick.

*Vidal* (Latin) "life."

*Vincent* (Latin) "conquering." Vin, Vince, Vincenz, Vinnie, Vinny.

*Virgil* (Latin) "blooming." Verge.

*Vito* (Latin) "alive." Vitus, Witold.

*Vladimir* (Slavonic) "world ruler." Valdemar.

*Volney* (Teutonic) "of the people."

*Wade* (Anglo-Saxon) "wanderer."

*Wainright* (Old English) "wagonmaker." Wayne, Wright.

*Waite* (Old English) "guard."

*Wakefield* (Old English) "from the wet field." Field, Wake.

*Waldemar* (Teutonic) "powerful and famous." Waldo, Wally.

*Walden* (Old English) "from the woods."

*Waldo* (Teutonic) "ruler." Familiar form of Oswald; Waldemar.

*Walker* (Old English) "thickener of cloth."

*Wallace* (Teutonic) "Welshman." Wallis, Wally, Walsh, Welch, Welsh.

*Walter* (Teutonic) "mighty warrior." Gauthier, Walt, Walther.

*Walton* (Old English) "from the walled town." Wally, Walt.

*Ward* (Teutonic) "guardian." Warden, Worden.

*Warner* (Teutonic) "guarding warrior." Werner.

*Warren* (Teutonic) "game warden." Waring.

*Washburn* (Old English) "from near the overflowing brook." Burn, Burnie.

*Washington* (Old English) "from the town known for astuteness."

*Watson* (Teutonic) "son of Walter."

*Wayland* (Old English) "from the land by the highway." Land, Way, Waylen.

*Wayne* (Old English) "wagoner." Short form of Wainright.

*Webster* (Old English) "weaver." Webb.

*Wells* (Old English) "dweller by the springs."

*Wendell* (Teutonic) "wanderer." Wende, Wendel, Wendelin.

*Wesley* (Old English) "from the western meadow." Lee, Leigh, Wes, Westley.

*Westbrook* (Old English) "from the western brook." Wes, West, Brook, Brooke.

*Weston* (Old English) "from the western farmstead." Wes, West.

*Wheeler* (Old English) "wheelmaker."

*Whitman* (Old English) "white-haired man." Whit.

*Whitney* (Old English) "from the white island." Whit.

*Whittaker* (Old English) "from the white field." Whit.

*Wilbur* (Anglo-Saxon) "beloved stronghold." Wilbert, Wilburt.

*Wiley* (Old English) "from the water meadow." Wylie.

*Wilfred* (Teutonic) "resolute and peaceful." Wilfrid, Will, Willie, Willy.

*Willard* (Teutonic) "resolutely brave." Will, Willie, Willy.

*William* (Teutonic) "determined guardian." Bill, Billy, Wilhelm, Will, Willi, Willie, Willis, Wilmer.

*Wilmont* (Teutonic) "beloved heart."

*Wilton* (Old English) "from the farm by the spring." Will, Willie, Wilt.

*Winfield* (Old English) "from the friendly field." Field, Win, Winnie, Winny.

*Winfred* (Teutonic) "friend of peace."

*Winslow* (Old English) "from the friend's hill." Win, Winnie, Winny.

*Winston* (Old English) "from the friendly town." Win, Winnie, Winny.

*Winthrop* (Old English) "from the friendly village." Win, Winnie, Winny.

*Witt* (Old English) "wise one." Witter, Wittier.

*Wolfgang* (Teutonic) "advancing wolf." Wolf.

*Woodrow* (Old English) "from the hedgerow in the forest." Wood, Woody, Woodward.

*Worth* (Old English) "from the farmstead." Worthington, Worthy.

*Wright* (Anglo-Saxon) "carpenter."

*Wyatt* (Old French) "guide."

*Wylie* (Old English) "charming." Lee, Leigh, Wiley.

*Wyman* (Old English) "warrior." Wymer.

*Wynn* (Old Welsh) "fair." Winnie.

*Xanthus* (Latin) "golden-haired."
*Xavier* (Arabic) "bright." Javier.
*Xenophon* (Greek) "strange voice." Zennie.
*Xenos* (Greek) "stranger."
*Xerxes* (Persian) "reuler." Zerk.
*Xylon* (Greek) "from the forest."

*Yakov* (Modern Hebrew) "a supplanter."

*Yale* (Old English) "from the corner of the land."

*Yancy* (Native American) "Englishman." Yance, Yank, Yankee.

*Yardley* (Old English) "from the enclosed meadow." Lee, Leigh, Yard.

*Yasir* (Arabic) "wealthy one." Yasah, Yursa, Yusri.

*Yates* (Old English) "from the gates of the settlement." Yeates.

*Yehudi* (Hebrew) "praise of the lord."

*York* (Old English) "estate of the boar."

*Yule* (Old English) "born at Yuletide." Yul.

*Yves* French form of Ivar. Ives.

*Zachary* (Hebrew) "remembered by the lord." Zach, Zachariah, Zacharias, Zacharie, Zak, Zeke.

*Zared* (Hebrew) "ambush."

*Zebulon* (Hebrew) "dwelling place." Zeb.

*Zedekiah* (Hebrew) "God is mighty and just." Zed.

*Zenas* (Greek) "living one." Zenon, Zenos.

*Zeus* (Greek) "great father of all."

*Zimri* (Hebrew) "celebrated in song."

*Zolly* (Hebrew) "form of Saul and Solomon.

*Zvi* (Hebrew) "deerlike." Zwi.

# Chapter 8

# *Birthstones And Flowers:*

## *What They Mean*

The Greek culture is responsible for the fascinating folklore that brings us birth gems and flowers. Exotic mythology surrounds these symbols; the wearing of one's birthstone was actually believed by the ancient Greeks to guard health and bring love and success in life.

If you need a gift idea for a new baby, why not present the child with a bouquet of his/her birth flowers, accompanied by a note explaining their significance (for the parents' benefit, of course)?

Here is the fun 'n fancy:

| MONTH | BIRTHSTONE | BIRTH FLOWER |
| --- | --- | --- |
| January | Garnet: symbol of constancy. The Greeks named this elegant fire-red jewel for the seeds of the pomegranate. | Carnation *(especially red)* |
| February | Amethyst: symbol of sincerity. This gem was said to be a favorite of both Cleopatra's and St. Valentine's. | Violet |
| March | Aquamarine: symbol of courage. | Jonquil |
| April | Diamond: symbol of love that stays young forever. The ancient Egyptians began the tradition of setting diamonds in their wedding rings. | Sweet Pea |
| May | Emerald: symbol of success. Even more than the diamond, this jewel has been a favorite of emperors and kings. | Lily of the Valley |
| June | Pearl: symbol of health. | Rose *(especially white)* |

| MONTH | BIRTHSTONE | BIRTH FLOWER |
| --- | --- | --- |
| July | Ruby: symbol of safety. The Greeks believed that "July children" wearing rubies could go anywhere and not meet harm. | Larkspur |
| August | Peridot: symbol of happiness. | Gladiolus |
| September | Sapphire: symbol of mental and moral well-being. Helen of Troy proudly displayed her beloved star sapphire. | Aster |
| October | Opal: symbol of hope. | Calendula |
| November | Topaz: symbol of fidelity. The Greeks believed "November babies" who wore the topaz would be graced with insight. | Chrysanthemum (*especially yellow*) |
| December | Turquoise: symbol of prosperity. The ancient persians wore this stone as an amulet to protect them; Southwestern American Indians also followed this tradition. | Narcissus |